Vegetable Gardening
with
Derek Fell

Vegetable Gardening
with
Derek Fell

Practical Advice and
Personal Favorites
from the Best-Selling Author
and Television Show Host

FRIEDMAN/FAIRFAX
PUBLISHERS

A FRIEDMAN/FAIRFAX BOOK

© 1996 by Michael Friedman Publishing Group, Inc.

Library of Congress Cataloging-in-Publication Data

Fell, Derek.
    Vegetable gardening with Derek Fell / written and photographed
by Derek Fell
      p.   cm.
    Includes index.
    ISBN 1-56799-253-6 (hardcover)
    1. Vegetable gardening.   I. Title.
SB321.F368   1996
635—dc20   95-49635
                                              CIP

Editor: Susan Lauzau
Art Director: Jeff Batzli
Designer: Susan Livingston
Photography Director: Christopher C. Bain
Production Coordinator: Marnie Ann Boardman

Color separations by Bright Arts Singapore Pte. Ltd.
Printed in China by Leefung-Asco Printers Ltd.

For bulk purchases and special sales, please contact:
Friedman/Fairfax Publishers
Attention: Sales Department
15 West 26th Street
New York, NY 10010
212/685-6610   FAX 212/685-1307

Dedication

For my three children, Christina, Victoria, and Derek Jr.,
all of whom love gardening.

Acknowledgments

In recent years I have enjoyed creating a series of twenty-five theme gardens at my home, Cedaridge Farm, in Bucks County, Pennsylvania, including a large vegetable garden. Nothing goes to waste. Anything that is not eaten fresh, my wife Carolyn makes into soup, or she finds ways to store it, usually by freezing or canning, so we have a continuous supply of our own highly nutritious, organically grown produce year-round.

The success of our vegetable garden, however, would not be possible without the help of my grounds supervisor, Wendy Fields, who ensures that the vegetable garden is always picture perfect.

Also, my sincere thanks to Kathy Nelson, my office manager, who helps keep my extensive photo library organized. Through her dedication to detail we maintain accurate records of everything that grows at Cedaridge Farm.

Contents

A little care will ensure a garden full of good-tasting vegetables such as these Egyptian-top onions (left) and 'Super-steak' tomatoes (above).

Introduction

I firmly believe that the first question a writer should address is his credentials, and also his reasons for writing a particular book. During the course of thirty years of photographing and writing about gardens I've authored or coauthored more than fifty books or calendars on all aspects of gardening, but nothing is closer to my heart than vegetable gardening. Indeed, the first book I ever wrote was on vegetable gardening—*Vegetables: How to Select, Grow and Enjoy* (HP Books)—a paperback that has sold close to 100,000 copies worldwide and is still in print after more than fourteen years.

There are a host of reasons why I grow vegetables—for one, I enjoy tastier, more nutritious food than I can buy at the local produce counter or even at a farm stand. By growing my own vegetables I can also be sure that the produce I eat is not contaminated with cancer-causing chemicals. Additionally, the process of cultivating a vegetable garden provides fresh air and exercise, along with a satisfying sense of well-being and pleasure at making something productive from a modest patch of bare soil.

An early book about vegetable gardening—written in the sixteeenth century—advised the reader to first fence in the garden, as a precaution not only against foraging animals but also from thieves! That's still good advice, but in my order of priorities for today's home gardener I would make that point number three. For modern gardeners, the most important considerations are variety selection and soil.

Variety Selection

My passion for vegetable gardening began in England when I started working for Hurst Seeds, which was at that time Europe's biggest seed house. I was responsible for producing its mail-order seed catalog, and I used to make frequent visits to its trial gardens in the Essex countryside, where I could evaluate the work of the resident vegetable breeder. The test gardens were extensive, and alongside vegetables bred by Hurst were those of competitive companies.

The breeder, George Beavin, would take me through his trials, and he once showed me a new lettuce called 'Buttercrunch', from Cornell University, which was the crispiest, tastiest variety he had ever grown. I remember him picking up a whole head, tearing it in half, and biting into the crunchy, yellow heart like an apple, offering me the other half. Indeed, to eat fresh lettuce like that in the middle of a vegetable plot was a revelation, and more than thirty years later I am still growing 'Buttercrunch'. He also showed me how his new 'Green Arrow' pea was capable of double the yields of older varieties, with up to twelve peas in a pod! I learned early that one of the most important aspects of vegetable gardening was variety selection.

No matter how good your soil, how ideal the site in terms of exposure to sunlight, or how often you fertilize or water during the season, you'll find that the result is only as good as the seed, and, in particular, the purity of the variety. Vegetable gardening is largely a matter of trust, since you cannot tell simply by looking at the seed whether it is first-rate or even viable. Its quality can be affected by many factors, including the origination of the seed, its longevity, conditions during storage, packaging, and other circumstances. I once bought a packet of carrots from an unfamiliar source, only to discover they were parsnips!

'Green Arrow' is one of the best pea varieties I have found. Don't underestimate the importance of selecting a variety that is suited to your soil and situation.

For peace of mind, my first rule of vegetable gardening is to buy seeds or plants only from reputable sources. Learn as much as you can about the seed companies of your choice. How long have they been in business? Do they have test gardens? Do they do any breeding work of their own? If possible, visit their test gardens and meet the staff. I put a lot of trust in varieties I have been successful with over a number of years, but I will experiment with a few newcomers if the catalog description is inspirational.

When I moved to the United States and began working with an American seed company, I quickly discovered that the varieties I had grown to like in England were mostly useless in North America. Britain has a maritime climate with mild winters, cool summers, and abundant rainfall; North America has a continental climate, with severe winters, hot summers, and often long periods of drought.

Planting varieties developed for your particular climate and growing conditions is critical. If you are new to vegetable gardening and want some good variety tips, go to a local farmer's market and ask experienced area growers what they recommend. I have been introduced to some wonderful varieties by word-of-mouth recommendations from growers who depend on results for a livelihood.

I also worked for three years as executive director of All-America Selections—the national seed trials. A seed-testing organization with a balance of academic and seed industry judges, All-America Selections has established a series of test gardens throughout the United States for making awards of recognition to flowers and vegetables, regardless of their origin. The only time I will trust a foreign-bred vegetable is if it wins an All-America Award, such as 'Yellow Baby' watermelon (developed in Taiwan), 'Melody' spinach (developed in Holland), and 'OS Cross' cabbage (developed in Japan).

Whenever I list a vegetable variety and recommend that you grow it, be assured that I have not only grown the variety myself, but have seen it under a number of conditions, know its pedigree, and often have visited with the breeder himself.

Seeds planted in good, well-prepared soil have the most favorable chance of growing into healthy, productive plants.

The Soil

After variety selection, the most important part of successful vegetable gardening is good soil. Get into the habit of conducting soil tests regularly (see Soil Testing on p. 25).

Scoop up a handful of soil and look at it closely, cupped in your hand. Poke it and crumble it. If you are like me, you will feel a sensation of power and the potential for miraculous growth. But if all you perceive is a boring clump of brown earth, think again! Good soil not only anchors plants, it provides them with essential nutrients. Though the nutrients may be there in granular form, plant roots absorb them in soluble form. Pieces of humus (decayed animal or vegetable matter) act like a sponge to hold moisture and dilute the nutrient granules so that plant roots can absorb them efficiently. Earthworms and beneficial soil bacteria are active in most soil, feeding on the humus and chelating particles of stone, then expelling them as nutrient-rich waste.

The worst thing you can do for your soil is rely on chemicals to control pests or provide food for plants. Even chemical fertilizers can produce a buildup of poisonous salts, depleting the populations of bacteria and restricting root development. I always strive for an environmentally safe answer to soil improvement and pest control—well-drained soils rich in humus and teeming with the beneficial bacteria that manufacture all the nutrients my plants will ever need. Even if my soil becomes infected with harmful soil nematodes or an unacceptable level of

When you grow vegetables organically, you can be sure that they are free of any chemical contaminants and safe for your family to enjoy.

harmful grubs, I will choose an organically approved method of soil purification (such as solarization, which uses a clear plastic sheet to bake the soil clean, or steam sterilization) rather than drench the soil with a chemical poison.

To be a good vegetable gardener is to be good at composting. If you have soil that is sandy or has a high clay content, then properly prepared garden compost will make a vast improvement. It can add body to a sandy soil, giving it moisture-holding ability. Compost will help break up dense clay soils, creating a crumbly texture that allows plant roots to penetrate freely. Well-made garden compost can also add nutrients that are released to plants slowly over an extended period, rather than in a flash like so many quick-acting packaged fertilizers. Compost can also help correct a soil that has a poor pH balance, bringing the pH closer to neutral, whether your soil is alkaline or acidic. Compost is especially effective when you create raised beds so that the compost rests above the impoverished existing soil.

I have been lucky. I was introduced to the benefits of vegetable gardening at an early age—in England—and now garden in what I consider the finest gardening climate of any in the world—Bucks County, Pennsylvania. In more than thirty years of gardening there has never been a year that I didn't plant a vegetable garden. Indeed, if I ever missed a season, I'm sure I'd feel that I had lost a year of my life!

Derek Fell
Cedaridge Farm
Gardenville, Pennsylvania

How to Plant a Vegetable Garden

There are sixteen basic steps for successfully growing a vegetable garden. In order of importance, these are:

I. Planning:

Layout, Seed Selection, and Transplants

My vegetable garden, at historic Cedaridge Farm in Bucks County, Pennsylvania, in early summer. As the season progresses, the sheep hurdles, used to fence out animals, also support pole beans.

Planning for a vegetable garden usually begins immediately after Christmas, when seed catalogs start to arrive in the mailbox. If you are not already on the mailing list of a mail order seed supplier, simply purchase a widely read gardening magazine, like *Organic Gardening* or *Horticulture,* and look for ads offering catalogs free of charge. Or, refer to the list of sources at the back of this book.

Even if you plan to buy some ready-grown transplants from a local garden center, you will still want a seed catalog to make good choices for certain plants, because vegetables like melons, squash, sweet corn, peas, and beans are all best grown from seeds rather than transplants. You will also find that local garden centers will install their new season's seed racks soon after January 1, offering enticing discounts for early bird buyers, but the choice is never so great from a seed rack as it is from a catalog.

To decide how many packets of seeds you will need and how many plants per row, make a plan on paper showing the dimensions of your plot. (The seed packet will tell you the spacing recommended, and whether the seed is best direct-sown or started indoors to obtain transplants). Use graph paper to lay out your garden, and allow each square to represent one square foot of garden space. Shown here are some sample layouts you can copy. The best is a "quadrant" design because it allows you to easily rotate crops in succeeding years. Crop rotation is essential to keeping your garden bountiful and disease-free, because plants like potatoes and cucumbers rarely do well two seasons in the same place.

Next, take some colored felt-tipped pens or crayons and use green to color in your cool-season crops—lettuce, spinach, broccoli, and cauliflower, for example. Then use red to mark your warm-season crops—tomatoes, sweet corn, and peppers, for example.

The most common mistake that beginning gardeners make is starting too big. Remember that a small space well cared for will generally outyield a large space that has been neglected. A good starter garden can be just 10 by 20 feet (3 by 6m); this manageable space can be mulched to keep down weeds and can be easily irrigated by a common lawn sprinkler during dry spells. A tiny vegetable plot that is regularly watered and kept weed-free can be amazingly productive, giving encouragement to try a larger size in subsequent years.

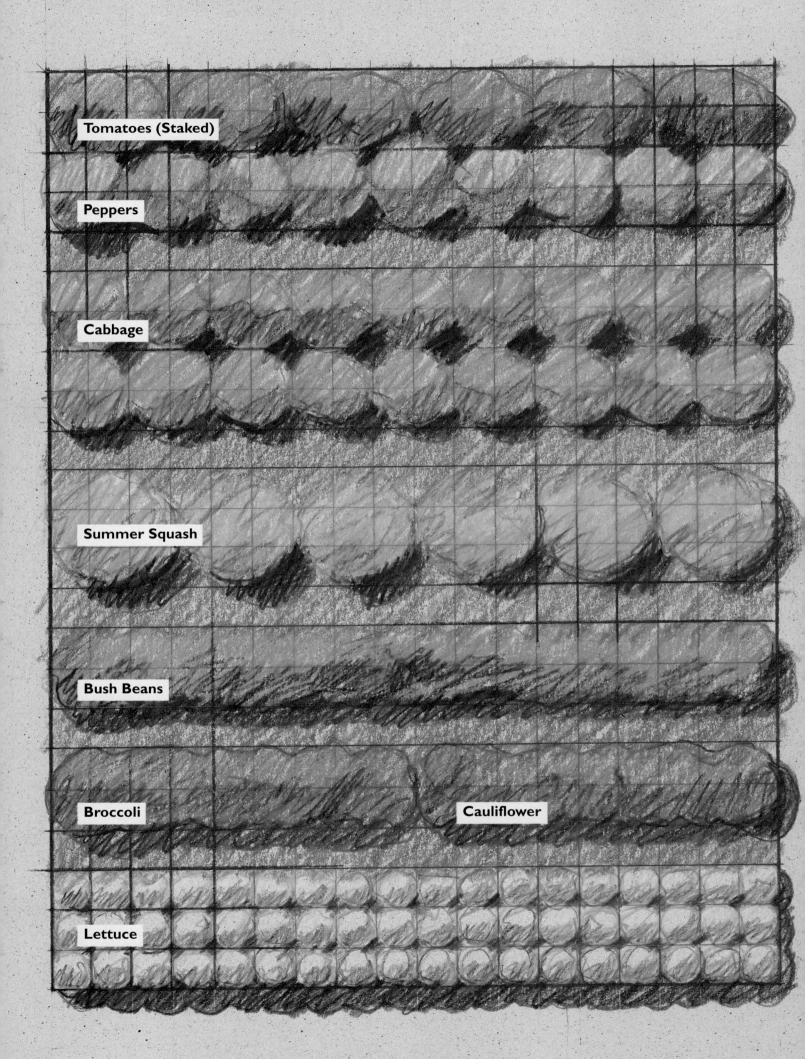

Your cool-season crops can be planted several weeks before your last expected frost date (even earlier if you grow them under plastic tunnels or floating row covers), while the warm-season crops must be planted after all danger of frost has passed.

After making a list of the varieties you want to grow, take a sheet of tracing paper and use it as an overlay to mark succession crops. For example, where the early, cool-season crop of spinach will be harvested by the end of spring, mark in a later-growing crop such as zucchini or bush beans so the space doesn't remain empty. This way you get maximum production from your plot.

Opposite: A simple, small-space planting plan for growing vegetables shows rows of staked tomatoes, peppers, cabbage, summer squash, bush beans, broccoli/cauliflower, and three rows of lettuce.

A lot of people are confused by the idea of rotation cropping. Because most gardeners have only a small space for a vegetable plot, they believe that they cannot provide a different location each year for each family of vegetables. If your space is limited, I suggest dividing your garden into quadrants, or squares, and rotating your crops in a clockwise direction each season. This way, the same vegetable will occupy the same space only once every four years. Marking a distinct and relatively permanent border between each quadrant is helpful when replanting each year. Edging each square of your garden with wooden boards is one solution.

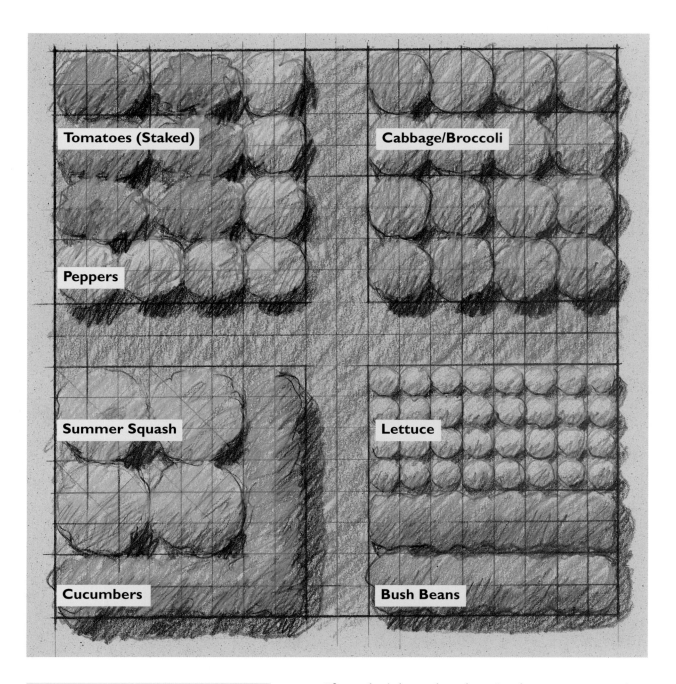

Tomatoes (Staked)

Peppers

Cabbage/Broccoli

Summer Squash

Lettuce

Cucumbers

Bush Beans

In a quadrant design, a square or rectangular plot is divided into four planting spaces by paths. This plan simplifies rotating crops from year to year.

If you don't know how long it takes to grow a particular crop, check the description in the catalog or on the seed packet. The description will tell you how many days are needed before you can harvest.

Once you've made your "wish" list, decide which varieties you want to grow from seed and which you prefer to grow from ready-grown plants. Many gardeners want to grow everything from seed because they have the patience and the facilities. Seed starting indoors is economical, but it requires bright light or an indoor lighting unit for good results. If you want to make starting your garden particularly easy, consider growing broccoli, cabbage, cauliflower, onions, peppers, and tomatoes from starter plants.

If space is at a premium in your vegetable garden, you may want to grow a heavy proportion of vining crops. Use trellises, tripods, or a fence to support vegetables such as pole beans, malabar spinach, tall peas, and even cucumbers, which have tendrils that allow them to climb unassisted. Most other vegetables will need to be tied to the supports. Vining vegetables generally have better flavor than dwarf, non-vining varieties, and of course, growing plants *up* allows you to make the most of space in even a tiny plot.

The most popular vegetables among home gardeners are tomatoes, snap beans, lettuce, zucchini squash, snap peas, peppers, broccoli, onions, carrots, and cabbage. These are all relatively high-yielding for the amount of space they occupy and are also easy to grow. Poorest yields per square foot (0.1 sq m) of space among popular vegetables are cauliflower (principally because it is somewhat sensitive to heat stress) and sweet corn.

For an extra-productive tomato patch that will keep on giving all season, consider growing three kinds: a cherry tomato like 'Sungold' hybrid (below), which ripens early and has good snacking flavor; a medium-size, everbearing, early variety like 'Early Cascade' hybrid (right), which produces red, round tomatoes; and a large-fruited variety like 'Big Boy' hybrid or 'Supersteak' hybrid (below right), both excellent for bragging about and for slicing into sandwiches.

When growing from seed remember that some vegetables, such as peppers and tomatoes, will need 6 to 8 weeks to make a sufficiently strong transplant. When ordering seeds, also check whether the seeds being offered are treated or untreated. Some seed houses will give you a choice, others will not. Treated seeds are dusted with a fungicide that inhibits rot; usually large-seed vegetables like sweet corn, peas, beans, and squash are treated. Organic gardeners don't like treated seeds, and instead sow untreated seeds extra thickly to compensate for any casualties due to fungus.

2. Location:

Sunlight, Drainage,
Shelter, and Water Source

This bountiful summer harvest is from my own garden at Cedaridge Farm.

The site selected for a productive vegetable garden should be in full sun—at least 6 hours is essential, and shade should not fall across the garden at the peak daylight hours, from about 11 A.M. to 3 P.M. If a tree shades any part of your garden space, prune away some limbs. Sometimes the removal of even a single branch can make a big difference.

The site should also have good drainage. If your chosen site doesn't drain well, consider digging a trench and laying some drainage pipe. If that sounds like too much of a chore, simply create some raised beds above the ground. Stones, bricks, untreated boards, and landscape ties all make excellent raised sides for the beds. Then bring in some good topsoil to fill them.

Sunlight is the key to high yields, and if you're lucky you will have a bright sunny spot where you can plant your vegetable garden. To determine whether you have enough sun to successfully grow vegetables, hammer wooden stakes into the ground around the perimeter of the proposed plot and connect them with string. Begin timing once the entire plot is free of shade and continue until shade once again begins to creep over the string: this is the number of hours that the space receives *direct sun*. Most cool-season crops (like lettuce and cabbage) will thrive on 6 hours of direct sun; most warm-season crops (like tomatoes) prefer a minimum of 8 hours for worthwhile yields.

You will also want to site your garden where you'll have easy access to water, preferably to a water spigot that can be used to run a garden hose and sprinkler or another system of dependable irrigation (see "Watering" on page 46).

This "edible landscape" features cabbages and other spring crops planted for ornamental effect as well as for produce.

If the site is flat, so much the better; if it happens to be on a slope too steep to cultivate, consider constructing a series of terraced beds. South-facing slopes are especially good places to grow vegetables if the soil can be held in place. Stone and brick terraces are the most aesthetically pleasing, but boards and railroad ties are less expensive.

Sheltered sites are also better than exposed, windy sites. If there is any danger of high winds or drift from salt spray, erect a temporary windbreak using bales of straw. The bales can be stacked to make a double or triple layer depending on the height of plants to be protected. However, planting wind-resistant hedges such as holly and Russian olive to act as a barrier is a better long-term solution.

To determine whether your intended garden site has the good drainage essential for most vegetable crops, dig a hole 6 inches (15cm) wide and 12 inches (30cm) deep, and pour in a bucket of water. If the water drains away within an hour, drainage is very good; if the hole is still mostly full after three hours, drainage is poor. If you need to use a site with poor drainage, consider installing drainage pipes or creating a raised bed, which will improve drainage.

If deer are a problem in your garden, think about erecting a deer fence of plastic netting stretched between posts. Deer fencing should be at least 4 feet (1.2m) high for a garden space less than 30 by 30 feet (9 by 9m); for a larger plot, the fence should be 10 feet (3m) high. Mesh fencing is about half as expensive as plastic-coated chain link, and is much easier and more cost-effective to replace if damaged. As an added bonus, the netting "disappears" into the landscape when the fence is viewed from a distance, and so is more attractive than many other utility fences.

Chain-link fencing coated with dark green plastic blends well with the surrounding plants and can be used as a support for vining vegetables.

If the site is accessible to thieves or foraging animals, fence it in. Inner-city gardens may need a cyclone wire fence with a locked gate to keep out vandals, while gardens in the suburbs and country may need fencing-in to deter rabbits, groundhogs, and deer.

3. Soil Testing:

Do-It-Yourself Kit versus Soil Laboratory Analysis

The degree of alkalinity and acidity in soil is known as its pH value. Soil too close to either extreme on the pH scale is detrimental to plants. The happy medium for most vegetables is soil that is either slightly acidic or neutral. If your soil is out of balance it will need conditioning to make amends.

You'll also need to know the amount of available nutrients (especially nitrogen, phosphorus, and potash) in your soil and how to correct any deficiencies.

Finally, you'll need to find out whether the soil has enough organic content, or humus. If it is too sandy or too clayey in texture it will need the addition of humus in the form of peat, well-decomposed animal manure, or garden compost.

It's a mistake to use a do-it-yourself soil test kit. Many of them only tell you the soil's pH, and even then the results can be hard to determine since they involve mixing some soil in a liquid and checking the color against a chart. Unfortunately, the color can be murky and difficult to match against any of the colors shown on the chart.

It's much better to go to a large garden center or your county agent's office and buy an inexpensive soil test kit that can be mailed to a soil test laboratory, usually located at your state university. The soil kit's instructions generally tell you to take teaspoonfuls of soil from twelve locations around your garden and place them in the pouch for mailing. Back comes a detailed analysis—usually a computer printout that tells you not only the pH of your soil, but how to correct it if there is an imbalance. Recommendations usually involve the addition of lime to make the soil less acidic or sulphur to make it less alkaline.

My son, Derek Jr., displays giant root crops—carrots, radishes, and beets—that have been grown using only organic gardening practices.

With a professionally tested soil sample, you will also learn how much of each essential nutrient is present and how to correct any deficiencies. If you plan to use only organic methods be sure to note this for the lab when you send in your soil sample.

The soil lab's printout will also tell you whether the soil needs the addition of humus and will advise you on the amount needed. You'll get different recommendations for different crops—a complete recommendation for vegetables, a different one for flowers, and one for orchard fruits, as well as a general purpose recommendation that covers all types of plants.

Many gardeners scoff at the idea of having their soil tested, and just work into the soil lots of garden compost on the theory that garden compost corrects all ills. Properly made, compost is extremely beneficial, but there is nothing like having an accurate soil analysis to tell you how to balance your soil and keep it in tip-top condition.

4. Site Preparation:

Clearing the Site and
Double Digging

When double digging, place the first spade depth of soil on a tarp before digging down a second spade depth.

Neatness counts a lot in a vegetable garden, and if you are planning to position your vegetable garden on a site that has lots of stones, trash, weed roots, or turf—or all of the above—then it is essential to remove these hindrances. My first recommendation is to completely remove the turf. Some gardeners say it's easier to till the site and plow the turf into the soil, but I don't like that shortcut because the turf is rarely completely covered and can soon reestablish itself. For a small garden space it doesn't take much effort to stake out your site with pegs and string, then take a flat-headed spade and scoop up squares of turf, relegating them to the compost pile.

You are then left with a cleared stretch of bare soil that needs digging. If you are planning to create substantial raised beds then you need to dig only to the depth of your spade, but if you want sensational results, or if you are going to cultivate on only slightly raised beds, then I suggest you dig down two spades deep. This is called double digging, and I have yet to see a gardening book explain how to double dig clearly. First, you need two large tarps (8' x 8' [2.4m x 2.4m] or larger). You lay these on either side of the bed you are digging, and you dig all the soil from the first level onto one tarp. You then dig all the soil from the next level onto the other tarp. The second layer of soil is usually not as good as the first—it is stony, and possibly filled with coarse roots or

As you fill in the top of the trench, mix humus—such as compost—into the indigenous soil (right). This is also a good opportunity to make use of any information received from soil tests to correct your soil pH. Then the site should be raked level before planting (below).

trash. As you are digging, toss stones, glass, and metal objects into a bucket or wheelbarrow and remove them. Simultaneously, into a separate wheelbarrow or bucket, toss roots and anything else that is woody. Burn the woody matter, placing the ashes onto your compost pile.

When you are finished double digging, you will be left with a wide trench approximately 2 feet (60cm) deep. Take a strong garden fork and fluff up the bottom soil, at the same time mixing in a 3- to 6-inch (7.5 to 15cm) layer of humus such as compost, peat, or well-decomposed animal manure.

Next, take the soil from the first layer and throw it back into the trench, also mixing in a 3- to 6-inch (7.5 to 15cm) layer of humus. Finally, take the soil from the *second* layer and use that to fill the remainder of the bed, not only mixing in a 3- to 6-inch (7.5 to 15cm) layer of humus, but also adding any soil conditioner that has been recommended by the soil test (such as lime for correcting acidity or sulphur for correcting alkalinity) and any fertilizer that has been recommended. It is most important that the fertilizer and soil conditioner be applied to the top layer because it is the surface roots of vegetables that are the most efficient in absorbing moisture and nutrients.

You will probably find that after all this digging you have more soil left over than you took out. That's good, because it means the new soil is full of air spaces and humus, creating a beautiful, crumbly, spongy medium for superb plant growth. The extra soil can be used to make the beds higher, dumped onto your compost pile, or used in other parts of the garden.

For larger sites you can rent a roto-tiller or hire a person with a roto-tiller to till your soil. In spring these workers-for-hire can be found in the classified section of your local newspaper. If the soil is poor, then spread a 6-inch (15cm) layer of compost over the site and allow the roto-tiller to mix it in. Good roto-tillers will chop even clay soil into fine pieces, leaving the site with a fine, crumbly soil texture.

Soil samples showing clay (top left), sand (bottom left), loam (bottom right), and humus (top right).

5. Soil Conditioning:

Sources of Humus

Soil conditioning is different from fertilizing. Throw fertilizer onto a sandy or clay soil, or onto highly acidic or highly alkaline soil, and it isn't going to do your plants much good. Soil conditioning isn't about *nutrients*, it's about *soil structure*—the ability of the soil to make nutrients available to plant roots and the ability of plant roots to penetrate the soil and absorb those nutrients.

Sandy soil is made up of large granules. It is full of air spaces, moisture passes through it quickly, it dries out quickly, and any nutrients are quickly washed away. To be truthful, sandy soil is not such a bad growing medium because it tends to heat up quickly in the spring (melons especially like warm, sandy soil), roots can probe through it quickly, and all that's really needed for a sandy soil is the addition of sufficient humus to give it the substance it needs to hold moisture and nutrients.

A well-made compost pile (above) consists mainly of shredded garden waste. Organic kitchen refuse (left) is also a good addition to compost piles. Together, these two ingredients break down into a moist, nutrient-rich soil conditioner.

Clay soils are composed of microscopic particles that bind together into impermeable lumps. Clay soils puddle water on their surface, are cold and sticky, and are heavy and awkward to dig. Adding sand doesn't help, but adding gypsum (a natural mineral that is also used to make plaster of paris) and humus breaks up the solids, provides air spaces, and allows roots freedom to spread. The quickest way to add humus to soil is with peat, which can be purchased in 50-pound (22.7kg) bales at local garden centers. This solution, however, tends to be expensive for large sites. Also on the negative side, there is no nutrient content to peat, and it normally needs the addition of fertilizer for good plant growth.

Garden compost—made from kitchen and garden waste piled up and allowed to decompose—can add not only humus but also nutrients, since wood ashes, eggshells, banana peels, grass trimmings, and shredded leaves combine to break down into a beautiful, fluffy, powdery soil rich in all the essential plant nutrients. Similarly, animal manures—especially well-decomposed stable and dairy manure—can provide both nutrients and humus. Another excellent source of humus is shredded leaves. Left for a year to break down into a loose, fluffy, dark brown earth, it turns into nutrient-rich leaf mold with ten times the moisture-holding ability of unimproved soil. Leaf mold is such a valuable soil conditioner that it pays to create a special bin from chicken wire to hold shredded leaves until they are ready for applying to the garden.

The best time to add soil conditioners is in autumn. At that time of year soil conditioners can be simply spread over the soil surface. Then in spring, at planting time, the conditioners can be raked, dug, or tilled into the soil.

6. Adjusting Soil pH:

To Lime or to Add Sulphur?

Lime raked into the upper soil surface of this newly dug bed will correct the high acidity, which was detected by a professional soil test.

Most unimproved soil tends to be heavily acidic or heavily alkaline. However, acidic soils can become alkaline by fertilizer abuse. Too much raw fertilizer leaves a salt buildup that can make acidic soil alkaline. To determine whether the soil's pH needs changing, refer to your soil test printout. If the acidity needs lowering the data will suggest how many pounds of lime to add to correct the imbalance, and if it's too alkaline the lab will normally advise you of how many pounds of sulphur to add.

Be aware that certain plants—such as blueberries—actually prefer a heavily acidic soil, but most vegetables grow well in a soil that is either neutral or only slightly acidic.

Soil tests conducted through a laboratory are ideal for determining the exact pH and nutrient requirements for your soil, but they can take time. If you want a quick way to check the pH levels in your garden, buy a pH meter from your local garden center. Stick its metal probe into several parts of your plot; a needle will instantly give a reading that shows whether your soil requires any amendment to make the pH suitable for growing vegetables.

7 . Digging:

To Dig or Not to Dig?

A fertile, well-drained soil is the foundation of a successful vegetable garden; soil must provide both anchorage and adequate nutrients.

The late Ruth Stout, a novelist and garden writer, popularized a method of gardening called the "no-dig" method. Once she had improved a space for growing vegetables by removing stones and fluffing up the soil she never dug it again—she simply piled compost on top of the soil like a mulch and planted through the top layer of compost. If the site is sheltered and free of foot traffic (including deer) then the soil never becomes compacted and the no-dig system works quite well.

However, deer trampling through a garden, as well as the action of sun, wind, rain, and snow, can cause soil compaction (especially on clay soils), so you should be prepared to dig the site over whenever it looks like the soil has become compacted. Once the site has been dug, never walk over it. If you must cross it for the purpose of raking or seeding,

Avoid compacting the soil when planting your newly dug vegetable garden by laying down long wooden boards to step on, rather than treading heavily onto bare soil. The boards will distribute your weight, preventing concentrated areas of compaction. However, be sure to take these boards up when you're not using them, since they can harbor colonies of destructive slugs and snails.

lay boards down so that the weight of your feet is distributed and somewhat cushioned.

The best tools for digging a small area are a shovel or spade. For spaces larger than 10 by 10 feet (100 square feet), consider renting a roto-tiller.

Left: My tool shed is host to a variety of useful gardening tools. Below: A small-size vegetable plot can be prepared using only a spade and a rake.

8. Raking:

Use the Front and the Back of the Rake

Seeds germinate best on a level surface and in fine, crumbly soil. The smaller the seeds (carrot seeds, for example), the more important it is to have a perfectly flat, fine-textured surface. The best tool for achieving this is a rake. First, rake the surface of freshly dug soil at an angle, removing stones and weed roots as the tines pick them up; then rake the soil over at the opposite angle to break the soil particles down even further. Finally, turn the rake over and use the flat side to make the soil surface as smooth as possible. In the process of using the back of the rake you will reduce the size of the soil particles even more.

If I am adding a granular organic fertilizer to the soil, I generally do it at the time of raking, to ensure that the fertilizer is worked into the upper soil surface.

This garden plot is being raked into wide, raised beds for extra topsoil depth and to improve drainage.

9. Fertilizing:

Chemical versus Organic, Granular versus Liquid, and Root versus Foliar Feeding

If you tried to live your life simply popping vitamin tablets, you would die a premature death. If you try to cultivate a vegetable garden relying entirely on packaged granular fertilizer, your plants can die. That's because there's more to nutrition than vitamins—other factors, like roughage, are essential to a healthy body. Humus is roughage for plants. Humus not only holds moisture like a sponge, allowing plant roots to absorb nutrients in liquid form, it provides aeration for the soil, so that plant roots can penetrate. It also serves as food for earthworms and beneficial microscopic soil organisms that ingest soil and expel it as waste, richer than when they ingested it.

Fertilizers come in many forms. They can be liquid or granular, slow-acting or fast-acting, chemical or organic. They can feed plants through their root systems and some can feed plants through their leaves (called foliar feeding). By law, packaged fertilizers must tell you what percentage of the contents are nutrients, and they are allowed to use the symbols N-P-K, meaning nitrogen, phosphorus, and potash. So, if you see an analysis on the bag that says 10-20-10 you know that 10 percent is nitrogen, 20 percent is phosphorus, and 10 percent is potash, making a total of 40 percent of the fertilizer plant nutrients. The rest (60 percent) is filler, included as a distributing agent.

You should realize that organic fertilizer formulations usually have a lower nutrient analysis for the same weight compared with chemical fertilizers, and release their nutrients more slowly. Some organic formulations can't even call themselves fertilizers, because they don't add enough nutrients to the soil. Instead they add enzymes that cause soil bacteria populations to explode, and their activity creates a natural increase in available plant nutrients.

Some fertilizers can be classified as either slow-acting or fast-acting. It's always best to choose a slow-acting fertilizer, as it remains active over a long period of time. Usually, one application of a slow-acting vegetable fertilizer is sufficient to last the season. It is particularly important that nitrogen be slow-acting. Phosphorus and potash tend to remain in the soil for extended periods, but nitrogen can be washed away quickly. Nitrogen is such an unstable plant nutrient, and can disappear from the soil so quickly, that soil test laboratories do not even test for it, but will give you a recommendation based on an assumption that the soil has none.

Fertilizer formulations may be in concentrated liquid form and need diluting with water. Others are in crystal form, and must likewise be mixed with water. Since every brand is different, you must read the label to determine

During the growing season, a foliar feed—which is absorbed through the plant's leaves—is an easy and effective way to give crops a fertilizer boost.

what the dilution rate should be. Fish emulsion is an example of a good organic liquid fertilizer. Applied to the root zone, it is good not only for initiating plant growth, but also as a booster application (again the product's label will explain how often to apply).

Some liquid formulations can also be applied to the leaves of plants. Research has shown, for example, that liquid fertilizers in a 1-2-1 ratio (such as 5-10-5) are especially good for foliar feeding fruiting vegetables. The high phosphorus content goes immediately to feed the flowers and immature fruit, producing giant-size tomatoes and peppers.

At Cedaridge Farm, we conscientiously add compost to the soil every spring, and we feed the soil with an or-

There are many organic feeding systems, which include both granular and liquid applications, that are available commercially. Note that organic fertilizers release nutrients more slowly and thus remain in the soil longer.

ganic formulation called Nitron, the brand name for a formulation that stimulates beneficial soil bacteria to manufacture plant nutrients. I prefer to use Nitron in its granular form, which looks and smells like oatmeal, but it can also be applied in liquid form.

Fertilizing is essential because vegetables are notoriously greedy feeders. It is generally insufficient to fertilize only once a season, unless you continually add garden compost to the soil's surface (called top-dressing). Because mulching and thick leaf cover can make applying granular fertilizer difficult, I recommend switching to a foliar feed as a booster, since vegetables will readily absorb nutrients through their leaves.

10. Planting:

Seed Starting and Transplanting

Many vegetables—cabbages and tomatoes, for instance—are best started from seed in individual peat pots and then transplanted into the garden when they're about 4 inches (10cm) tall.

Basically, you have two choices at planting time—seeding directly into the garden (a one-step operation, since the seeds are planted directly into a furrow and covered over in one easy step) or transplanting seedlings you have either started from seed indoors or purchased as "starts" from a garden center. With many fast-growing, large-seeded vegetable varieties—like beans and sweet corn—direct seeding is best. You simply make a furrow with a trowel and place the seeds at the proper depth in rows spaced the required distance for the particular vegetable or variety. Some small-seeded vegetables—like carrots and turnips—are better off when direct seeded because they resent any kind of root disturbance.

If you ever encounter problems (such as poor seed emergence) from direct seeding, consider sowing pregerminated seeds. This involves "sowing" seeds indoors on a moist paper towel and keeping them warm and moist until the seeds are germinated. Then simply take the paper towel into the garden and place each germinated seed into its growing position, covering lightly with soil. By speeding up the emergence of the embryo you also lessen the chances of the seedling dying from rot and soil-borne diseases.

Vegetables that need a long time to mature, like tomatoes and peppers, are best started indoors up to 8 weeks before outdoor planting, or purchased as ready-grown

It's most economical to buy seeds packaged in seed packets. Seed tapes and other convenience methods of packaging seeds are usually just gimmicks. The tapes are not as easy to lay as the package promises, and you may be left with wide gaps in your row if some of the prespaced seeds fail to germinate. Among conventional seed packets, those that have foil pouches within the paper packet assure the highest rate of germination and the longest storage, since natural aging of the seeds begins only when the foil is opened. High heat and humidity can age seeds quickly, so to preserve the viability of seeds packaged in paper alone, store the packets in the vegetable bin of your refrigerator until you're ready to sow them. Transfer any leftover seeds into small glass jars and add a tablespoon of baking soda to help keep the seeds dry.

transplants. Remember, though, that when you rely on ready-grown transplants, your choice of varieties is much more limited than when you start your own plants from seed.

If you want to save money and grow your own transplants you'll need a place with good overall light. Greenhouses and sunrooms with overhead skylights are excellent for starting seeds; windowsills tend to have directional light, so it may be necessary to place a reflector—such as a white card or a sheet of aluminum foil—on the low-light side to bounce light into the poorly lit areas. Also, to prevent the seedlings from stretching toward the light, which weakens them, you may need to elevate seed trays at least to the level of the window pane.

Where natural light sufficient for seedling growth is a problem, consider an indoor light unit. The best ones have adjustable lights and room for several tiers of plants, with directions on how high above seed trays to set the lamps and how long to keep the lights on for successful germination.

There are many types of containers that can be used to start seedlings, but basically they fall into two groups: containers that are appropriate for the two-step method and those that are best for the three-step method (remember, direct seeding is a one-step operation but it's not suitable for all vegetables.)

The two-step method involves peat or plastic pots filled with a soil mix or expandable peat pellets—such as Jiffy-7 peat pellets—that swell up with water. You simply sow a group of seeds in the top of the moist soil and, once they've germinated, thin to one strong seedling. When it's large enough to transplant (usually 4 inches high) transfer the plant directly into the garden. If the pot is made of plastic, you must slide the root ball carefully out of the pot and place the root ball into the garden soil with as little root disturbance as possible. With peat pots, you can simply tear out the bottom of the pot to release the roots. If you're using peat pellets you should carefully remove any netting; otherwise the plants may stay root-bound. Tomatoes, peppers, cabbage, and melons are good to start using the two-step method.

The three-step method requires the extra step of germinating in a seedling tray. Seedling trays are usually peat or plastic containers filled with potting soil; seeds are then scattered over the surface. As the seeds germinate and produce a pair of leaves they are lifted carefully and transferred to an individual peat or plastic pot. When plants are large enough to transplant into the garden the treatment is the same as for the two-step method. Again, make sure that the root ball is not disturbed. Lettuce, spinach, and chard are good to start using the three-step method.

The four seed trays in the center are topped with plastic covers, which retain moisture and speed germination.

f you have had difficulty germinating certain seeds by direct-sowing (for instance, if you have poor stands of spinach, peas, or corn), you may hear recommendations to use "chitted" seeds. Chitted seeds are simply seeds that have been pregerminated. These chitted seeds are then sown into furrows in the gar-

den. Any seeds that fail to swell should be discarded, as they are probably not viable, but sow all swollen seeds, even those that have not split their coats and produced a root. This technique allows seeds to emerge from the soil quickly and reduces the risk of wide gaps along rows, since you can be certain that all seeds sown are viable. Chitting is particularly advisable with hybrid seeds, since the seed count for hybrids is generally low and the seeds are more expensive than nonhybrid varieties.

When starting seeds in seed trays, be sure to label the trays with the variety name, the source of the seeds, and the date of sowing. Always use a sterile potting soil to avoid fungal diseases.

It is most important that seedling trays or pots not be allowed to dry out. Direct sunlight shining through a south-facing window can quickly evaporate soil moisture and kill plants from dehydration. Water seeds with a mister, since running water from the spout of a watering can may disturb the soil surface and prevent seeds from germinating.

Perhaps the greatest danger to seedlings is a fungal disease called damping-off disease, which attacks seedlings at the soil line, causing them to keel over and die. It is a frequent occurrence when plants are started indoors using contaminated soil or pots that have not been thoroughly cleaned before reuse.

This frame is designed to support a covering of clear plastic, giving an early planting of tomatoes protection from frost. If you set plants out early, stay tuned to the weather so that you can shelter crops when necessary.

The best indicator of a healthy candidate for transplanting is a compact, bushy green plant. Any kind of stress—such as inadequate light, irregular watering, overcrowding, or pest damage from spider mites or aphids—usually shows itself by yellowing of leaves, stretching, and a wilted appearance. Also, remember that plants that are not in bloom (especially tomatoes and peppers) are less likely to suffer from transplant shock.

Be prepared for unexpected frosts. Listen to weather forecasts and if there is any danger of a late frost, cover the rows of transplanted seedlings. Indeed, it is often possible to get an earlier than usual start to the season by planting early and having handy some moveable plastic tunnels or plastic cages to cover plants whenever the air temperature turns too cold.

Plants must be gradually acclimated to their new conditions before they make the transition from a warm, protected environment to the outdoors. Keep the plants in a

Saving seeds from the hybrids you grow is ill-advised, since the next generation usually loses vigor and produces inferior results. Also, repeatedly saving seeds from nonhybrid, or open-pollinated, varieties can also lead to problems since diseases can be transmitted through the seed (lettuce is so susceptible to seed-borne diseases that lettuce seed growers ensure healthy seed crops by planting in special valleys isolated from disease contamination). For a strain to remain pure, many seed crops must be isolated from cross-pollination and "rogued," to eliminate off-types. The easiest seeds to save are those of large-seed varieties such as peas, beans, and nonhybrid corn.

cold frame (or under a make-shift plastic shelter) for several days so they become conditioned to colder temperatures. This is known as *hardening-off.* This way, the plants do not suffer transplant shock, and if a cold spell occurs they are protected. Hardening-off is very important for tender, warm-weather plants like tomatoes and peppers, but even hardy plants like cabbage and broccoli will benefit.

The use of floating row covers (a lightweight horticultural fabric that covers plants like a spider's web) is also a good tool for protecting plants from cold spells. I'll discuss floating row covers further in the section on pest control (see page 48).

Above: A raised bed of seedling lettuces has been hardened-off to condition them to the cooler temperatures of the outdoors. Left: Upturned peach baskets can protect tender plants from light frosts.

II. Thinning:

Be Cruel to Be Kind

There are ways to avoid thinning, which I will explain, but with certain root crops like carrots it's hard to get maximum yields from minimum space without the tedious chore of hand thinning. Besides, even with seeds that are easy to handle (like cucumbers and melons, which can be spaced at precise distances to avoid thinning) I often overseed in order to compensate for any unforeseen losses (from rot or slugs, for instance).

Some vegetables, like leaf lettuce, will tolerate crowding, so rigorous thinning isn't necessary, but when plants such as beets, turnips, and head lettuce are crowded, thin-

Above: Rows of radish seedlings are thinned to ensure that the roots do not crowd each other. Right: A "hill" full of cucumber seedlings should be thinned down to several plants.

ning is essential. The time to thin plants is as soon as the seedlings begin to emerge through the soil. The most important caution with thinning is not to disturb the seedlings you want to remain. This is very difficult with tiny seedlings like carrots and beets, so a good tool to use is a pair of scissors with a sharp point. By cutting off the unwanted seedlings at the soil line you will not disturb the rest of the row.

Psychologically, it's hard for many people to thin plants, so I'll discuss some alternatives to thinning. You can buy pelleted seed from some companies so that tiny seeds are easy to space at the correct distance. Also, seeds like carrot can be purchased in seed tapes, with the seeds at pre-measured distances. The trouble with seed tapes is that they allow no room for unforeseen hazards that can produce low germination (such as damping-off disease, which can be caused by any of several fungi, and affects seedlings just after they emerge from the soil).

A better way to avoid thinning is to mix fine seeds with sand so that you have a distributing agent that separates the seeds. But my favorite no-thinning trick is to pregerminate seeds in a moist paper towel, and plant the germinated seeds at precisely the right distances. This works well with fine seeds like carrots, and I also use this method with peas and lima beans because they are susceptible to rot. Inadequate moisture and too low a soil temperature are also common causes of seeds failing to germinate; pre-germinating will allow you to control moisture and temperature and assure that the seeds germinate.

12. Weeding:

Mulch, Mulch, and More Mulch

Spinach planted through black plastic lines wide, raised rows. A drip irrigation system underneath the plastic keeps the plants well watered.

More vegetable gardeners abandon their plots through problems with weeds than for any other reason. Early in the season it's relatively easy to pull any weeds that spring up between rows, but during the summer, and especially when there have been thunderstorms to charge the soil with moisture and nitrogen, even a week of neglect is likely to result in a tangle of weeds that can strangle your vegetables and prove difficult to eradicate.

The easiest way to get rid of weeds is to mulch—to apply a covering over the soil that allows your cultivated crops to grow, but that effectively suffocates weeds. The most appealing mulches are organic mulches such as shredded leaves, grass clippings, straw, and pine needles. However, be aware that these organic mulches have a tendency to cool the soil. They are fine for cool-season crops like broccoli, cauliflower, lettuce, and cabbage, but they can inhibit the growth of tomatoes, melons, and peppers in northern climates. A far better mulch for warm-season crops is black plastic, because it is not only a completely effective barrier against weeds, it has a tendency to warm the soil early and keep it warm all through the growing season. If you don't like the look of black plastic or if you live in a hot climate, where black plastic would cook the soil, then by all means cover the plastic with an organic mulch after the soil has warmed. That's what I do. Also, it's important to reapply mulch if it becomes thin. Organic mulches especially are easily dissipated from the action of wind, rain, and decomposition. When weeds start to break through, add more mulch.

Winter cleanup is also important for the control of weeds. Some weeds will break through the mulch and experience a spurt of growth in autumn that allows them to form seeds. Go through the garden periodically and pull out all weeds before they have a chance to set seeds, and either burn them or add them to the compost pile. Also, mulches can harbor harmful pests and fungal diseases during winter, so it is always a good policy to rake up organic mulches in autumn and burn them or toss them onto the compost pile. Then I like to take up all the black plastic and run a three-pronged hoe through the soil so the plastic doesn't become a breeding ground for pests like slugs during winter.

The application of black plastic requires care. Since rolls of black plastic are commonly sold in 3-foot (90cm) widths, it makes sense to build your rows up into 2-foot (60cm)-wide raised beds, with a 4-inch (10cm) rise above

I use wood chips in my vegetable garden— shown here in early spring—to create clean, weed-free pathways clear of mud.

the surrounding soil, leaving 2 inches (5cm) on either side to anchor the plastic with soil. It is extremely important to anchor the sides of the plastic; otherwise, wind can blow under the flaps and tear it apart.

Lay the plastic before you start planting. Using a yardstick, measure off planting stations, then cut an X with a pair of scissors for seeds or transplants. With compact vegetables like lettuce and cabbage you can usually crowd two rows of plants along a 2-foot (60cm)-wide bed. Smaller plants like onions will allow you to fit four rows, while larger plants like tomatoes will only allow one row.

13. Watering:

The Joys of Drip Irrigation

Above left: This drip irrigation system, which can be left in place for several seasons, was made from recycled automobile tires. Above: A lawn sprinkler system waters a bed of lettuce.

A reliable source of water is needed at all stages of growth in a vegetable garden—from germination to the point of harvesting. Seeds need water to germinate and grow. If they are deprived of moisture soon after germination they can wither and die even before they poke their heads through the soil.

People like to have a drink of water every day. So do plants! Research has shown that, providing the soil drains well, the ideal for almost all vegetables is a drink of water every day. But that's not always easy to manage. At the very least, supplemental water should be provided whenever a week goes by without an inch of natural rainfall. Also, there are phases of a plant's growth when water is particularly essential—for example at the time of tasseling for sweet corn (that's when pollination occurs and the ears start to swell their kernels) and at time of fruit formation for tomatoes (that's when the growing fruit is most susceptible to blossom-end rot disease, a calcium deficiency caused by inadequate watering).

Aside from natural rainfall, there are basically four ways to water a vegetable garden: by using a watering can, which is okay for watering a small-scale planting like a cluster of container plants on a patio; with a watering hose, which is also fine for small-scale plantings; with a lawn sprinkler, which is good for larger areas, since the sprinkler can be left on overnight to give the garden a thorough soaking; and through drip irrigation, which can be used for watering small-, medium-, and large-sized spaces at the turn of a faucet.

Without doubt, the best investment a gardener can make after buying quality seed is to install a drip irrigation system that releases the gardener from any dependence on natural rainfall, and puts the water exactly where it's needed—directly at the root zone.

There are many brands of drip irrigation systems, and I've tried them all. There are basically two kinds available: hoses that "sweat" moisture all along the line and hoses that have emitters spaced along the line. Forget the emitters—they always clog. Opt for a system that sweats moisture all along the line, either a throw-away system like Irrigro, which is inexpensive enough to be used for one season, then discarded, or a system like Leaky-Hose, which uses longer-lasting rubber hose made from recycled automobile tires.

Drip lines are laid down the center of wide raised rows before planting. This easy-to-install system will free the gardener from worry during dry spells.

Drip irrigation systems are especially good for use under mulches because the mulch will help protect them from damage. Some models incorporate an automatic fertilizing system, so a pellet of fertilizer is mixed with the water as it goes through the line. Others feature a timing device that turns the water on at pre-set intervals so you can go away on vacation for several weeks and have your garden watered.

Right: A black plastic watering tray warms the soil for tomatoes. Below: A wire cage protects greens from foraging animals.

14. Pest and Disease Control:

Organic versus Chemical

The first rule of pest and disease control is crop rotation. Move your plant families around so you never grow the same crop in the same spot two years in succession. The second rule is soil maintenance. Fertile, well-conditioned soil supports vigorous plants that are able to resist pests and diseases better than weak ones. The third rule is proper cleanup. Always clean up the garden in autumn. Pull out dead plants by their roots, burn or compost weeds and old mulch, and pick up loose boards, discarded bricks, and sheets of plastic, which can shelter pests and diseases.

The further south you live the worse pests and diseases seem to be. Pesky insects like army worms and nematodes, and virulent fungal diseases like verticillium wilt and anthracnose, seem to thrive in warm, humid climates. In the South, pests can reach plague proportions and destroy a crop before it comes to maturity.

The larger the pest the easier it is to control. Deer, woodchucks, and rabbits can be fenced out of a vegetable plot, but no matter how hard you try you will never completely rid your garden of flea beetles or mildew diseases spread by microscopic spores.

Lots of pests can be controlled by hand. Just go out into your garden every day, and if you see signs of slugs put on a glove and pick them off in the early morning when silvery trails mark their whereabouts. As soon as Japanese beetles make an appearance do the same. And if aphids start to colonize plant stems blast them off with a jet of water.

However, the most effective way of guarding crops against pests and diseases is with floating row covers. Floating row covers are constructed of a lightweight fabric that rests on top of plants to form a tunnel. The sides are anchored to the soil with pegs or stones. The fabric is sufficiently transparent to allow plenty of light to pass through, and as the plants grow they push the fabric up. Deer will not chew through floating row covers and even small pests like flea beetles cannot penetrate the fabric barrier. These covers are especially good at protecting compact crops like cabbage, lettuce, and bush beans.

These "scare-eye" balloons, hung at intervals throughout the garden, are effective for controlling damage from birds, especially crows.

Whatever problems occur, never resort to chemical controls. The risk of poisoning the land or yourself is too great, even if you follow application instructions precisely. The very act of breathing in residue from chemical sprays or having them touch your skin may have costly long-term effects.

There is a lot of controversy in the gardening community over what constitutes an organic remedy. For example, some organic purists will not recognize either rotenone or pyrethrum as organic pest controls since they are harmful to

A wooden, A-frame trellis helps support disease-resistant cucumbers. Choosing varieties that are resistant to diseases is one of the best organic methods for producing healthy vegetables.

beneficial insects also. I use them because they are made from the powdered parts of plants and once they come into contact with soil the active ingredients decompose into harmless particles. However, they are not selective in their effect. In other words, some beneficial insects (such as butterflies) are endangered along with the target pest, though the number of beneficial insects endangered in the confines of a vegetable garden is likely to be negligible. Also, both rotenone and pyrethrum are toxic to fish and are potentially hazardous if ingested by humans.

A more widely praised target pest control is BT, short for *Bacillus thuringiensis,* a biological control that works well on caterpillars, grubs, and other larvae of moths and butterflies such as the cabbage white butterfly, which can do tremendous damage to cabbage crops. It will still kill a few beneficial insects such as swallowtail butterfly larvae, but these beneficial insects are mostly born beyond the confines of a vegetable garden. Different strains of BT attract different target groups (for example, BT San Jose destroys Colorado potato beetle larvae).

A good way to control diseases organically is by choosing disease-resistant varieties. For example, many tomatoes, such as 'Supersteak' hybrid, are resistant to both verticillium and fusarium wilt, as well as to harmful soil nematodes. Certain cucumbers, such as the 'Marketmore' strains, are resistant to the most common cucumber diseases, and 'Stonehead' cabbage has extremely good resistance to black rot. Certain peas, such as 'Knight', are resistant to several troublesome pea diseases.

15. Harvesting:

Tips for Flavor and Productivity

An abundant harvest of Swiss chard and Irish potatoes, including yellow, red, and blue varieties, is ample reward for a season of vegetable gardening here at Cedaridge Farm.

In general, it's best to harvest from your garden in the morning and to cover harvested fruits with a wet cloth to protect them from dehydration, since some vegetables—like lettuce and sweet corn—can lose their crispness or start converting sugars to starch as soon as they are picked.

Make a habit of harvesting for a particular need. Any blemished tomatoes, for example, may be fine for fresh salads because the blemished parts can be cut out and discarded. Blemish-free fruits should be used for canning. Similarly, when harvesting carrots you might want to separate them into two groups—those with split or wormy roots and those that are blemish-free. Use the flawed roots for fresh eating and the perfect ones for dry storage, canning, or freezing.

The nuances of harvesting particular vegetables will be discussed in detail in the A-to-Z listing of vegetables.

Too many vegetables? My favorite method of storing surplus vegetables is to blend them all together into a soup, and then freeze the soup. I like to use the no-fuss plastic freezer cartons that are available in any supermarket. It's also easy to preserve vegetables separately by freezing them, but be aware that different vegetables require different methods of preparation in order to kill potentially harmful bacteria. There are several excellent books on the market that provide step-by-step instructions for freezing produce safely. If you are still overwhelmed by the bounty of your garden, there are organizations all across the country that will take surplus produce to feed the hungry.

16. Succession Planting:

Follow Cool-Season Crops with Warm-Season Crops

When an early crop is finished bearing rip it out by the roots, compost the stems, aerate the soil, add a little compost or fertilizer, and replant the space with another crop—preferably one from a different plant family than the one you have just uprooted. For example, lettuce and peas are often finished by the end of June, as hot weather exhausts them. By removing the spent plants entirely, a succession crop of a fast-growing warm-season vegetable is possible (such as zucchini or cucumbers, which are from an entirely different plant family). When the zucchini are finished, you may even be able to grow a third crop, such as bush beans. The practice of following a spent crop with a new succession planting ensures maximum use of available space.

Most years I am able to enjoy three plantings of bush beans, with the first sowing in late April, the second in early July, and the third in mid- to late August.

Make the most out of your garden space with succession plantings. By following a cool-season crop (like lettuce) with a warm-season one (like zucchini squash), you'll get twice the yield from the same space. But there is a bit of preparation for the second planting. A soil depleted of nutrients from an early crop will usually produce poorly for a succession crop unless the soil is aerated and fed anew. Immediately after clearing an early crop, fluff up the soil with a cultivator or a spade, and rake in some good garden compost or granular fertilizer. Avoid following an early crop with a repeat sowing of the same or a similar crop (for example, radishes are a poor choice to follow cabbages since both are cole crops), as disease will usually take its toll on the second crop.

Vegetables In Containers

The big benefit of growing plants in containers is that you can change the soil every year. This way, you never get a buildup of soil pests and diseases and you don't need to practice crop rotation like you do with plants grown in a plot. Secondly, if you use a container with good natural insulation, like wood or clay, you will not have the overheating of the soil that plagues many container-grown plants—especially those grown in plastic and metal containers. Finally, it is important to be aware that sturdy stakes are necessary to support luxurious vine growth and heavy crops of bountiful fruit. Without strong supports such as bamboo poles, plants are likely to topple over and uproot themselves from the soil.

Soil for containers should be equal parts of humus (such as peat or garden compost), screened topsoil, and sand (but not beach sand, which contains salt). It's easiest to blend these ingredients together on a tarp, making enough to do all the containers you plan to fill. The soil must be fertile: add a 5-10-5 granular fertilizer and limestone to the soil mix (the quantities depend on the amount of potting soil you plan to make; calculate the amount by following label instructions). Water daily and fertilize with a mild-strength liquid fertilizer weekly. When days are hot and humid, hose the plants down—this is most important if your containers are surrounded by brick or flagstone, as on a terrace or patio.

Following is a list of vegetable varieties that are especially good for growing in containers.

• *Bean, 'Roma II'* (53 days) The bush form of famous pole bean '*Romano*' needs no support and produces loads of flat, edible pods with a tender, melt-in-the-mouth flavor. This variety easily produces fifty beans to a plant. Set as many as four plants around the edges of a 3-gallon container.

• *Cucumber, 'Bush Champion'* (55 days) This variety produces slicing cucumbers up to 11 inches long on compact vines. You can expect a dozen quality cucumbers per plant in a 3-gallon container, especially if you provide a short trellis to hold the vine upright.

Above: Compact-vine 'Pixie Hybrid' tomatoes are ideal for growing in pots. Below: Colorful 'Rainbow' chard makes a highly decorative container plant, and has the advantage of lasting all season.

• *Eggplant, 'Dusky Hybrid'* (65 days) These are pear-shaped, medium-sized, glossy black fruits on bushy plants. This variety easily produces a dozen hefty fruits in a 3-gallon container.

• *Lettuce, 'Tom Thumb'* (70 days) This miniature head lettuce needs only 4-inch (10cm) spacing. It is best grown in a windowbox planter, or in a dish planter that allows six to eight heads per container.

• *Pepper, 'Sweet Banana'* (72 days) An upright plant, 'Sweet Banana' pepper produces up to fifty crisp, sweet, elongated fruits in a 3-gallon container. Harvest them at different stages of ripeness—green, yellow, orange, and red.

• *Pepper, 'Little Dipper'* (66 days) A miniature bell pepper that quickly turns red and stays red for weeks, this variety grows to just 26 inches (66cm) high. It is exceedingly decorative, even in a gallon container.

• *Swiss Chard, 'Rainbow'* (60 days) This multi-colored variety tolerates crowding. Four plants will grow in a 3-gallon container.

• *Tomato, 'Pixie Hybrid'* (52 days) The fruits are larger than cherry size, have a "big tomato" flavor, and are ideal for slicing into salads. 'Pixie' is the earliest tomato you can grow, ripening in just 52 days from transplants, beating even cherry tomatoes.

• *Zucchini Squash, 'Goldrush'* (50 days) This all-female variety will produce dozens of golden yellow fruits in a 3-gallon container.

The Best
Vegetables
to Grow

> **The beautiful crimson head of grain amaranth becomes loaded with nutritious, nutty seeds that may be roasted in a skillet until they pop like popcorn. This plant is very easy to grow, and is both heat- and drought-tolerant.**

Amaranth,

Grain & Quinoa

Amaranth and quinoa are very similar in appearance, though amaranth is much easier to grow because it matures earlier and tolerates hot, dry growing conditions. Chances are good that you have never even seen or eaten either grain amaranth or quinoa. Both are very beautiful plants, with large, colorful seed heads in red, pink, and yellow, and their edible seeds are extremely tasty when properly prepared.

If you want to try grain amaranth, go to your local health food store and purchase a box of amaranth cereal. You'll find it crunchy and nutty—probably the best dry cereal you ever tasted. The Rodale Research Institute is largely responsible for introducing grain amaranth into home gardens, and Seeds of Change, a New Mexico seed company, is largely responsible for introducing quinoa, which is not as widely adaptable as amaranth because of its preference for cool nights. Nor is quinoa quite so easy to prepare, because it has a bitter coating around the seeds which must first be removed. Amaranth and quinoa were both food staples of the Mayan and Inca civilizations.

Plants of both grain amaranth and quinoa grow to 6 feet high in one season, and take 100 days to mature. Sow the seeds directly into the garden, about half an inch deep. Thin seedlings to stand at least 12 inches (30cm) apart with 2 feet (60cm) between rows. Chewing insects like Japanese beetles can be a problem, so control these by using milky spore bacterial control or beetle traps.

To harvest amaranth, cut down the seed heads after frost kills the lower stem section, then dry and thresh the seed heads, removing any small twigs or leaves. Pour some cooking oil in a skillet as you would to prepare popcorn, and lightly stir until seeds pop. The popped grain may be eaten as a snack or cooked in water (1 cup of grain to 3 cups of water) for 20 minutes to make a hot cereal.

For quinoa, thresh the seeds and separate them from the chaff. Rinse the seeds thoroughly until the bitter coating around the seeds is removed completely, then cook 1 cup of grain in 3 cups of water for 20 minutes.

Leaf amaranth is highly decorative and makes a good heat-resistant substitute for spinach. The young leaves are edible when raw, and can be added to salads or used as a garnish; more mature leaves are best boiled or steamed for a side dish.

Amaranth,
Leaf

Leaf amaranth is useful as a substitute for spinach. It tolerates hot weather better than spinach and it is much more compact than the grain amaranths, growing just 3 feet (90cm) high. Depending on the variety, the leaves can be plain green or multicolored like coleus, with combinations of yellow, red, and maroon in the younger leaves. The top whorl of leaves is the tastiest—they can be either cooked like spinach or shredded raw into salads. 'Tampala' (50 days) is a variety that freezes well and shrinks very little on cooking. 'Joseph's Coat' is a vivacious multicolored variety. Space leaf amaranth plants 12 inches (30cm) apart in rows spaced 2 feet (60cm) apart.

Artichoke

Artichokes are the immature flower buds of a type of giant thistle native to the Mediterranean. Plants that are treated to a long, cool growing season can yield up to fifty edible chokes.

Unless you live in a fairly frost-free coastal climate, artichokes are a challenge to grow. Artichokes are perennials, and need a long growing season, along with fertile soil and regular amounts of moisture, to produce worthwhile yields.

Artichokes are fancy thistles from the Mediterranean, and the edible part is a large, scaly flower bud that will open into a gigantic purple thistle if not harvested. Take care handling artichokes—even the head can have sharp spines at the tips of each scale. To render artichokes edible you should pick them with about one inch of stem attached, cut the spines off the scales with scissors, and immerse the entire head in boiling water for 30 to 40 minutes, depending on its size. To test for tenderness poke the inch of stem with a fork and if the fork sinks in easily the cooking is complete. Eat the artichoke leaves by peeling away the scales, dipping the base in butter, and scraping the tender part between your teeth.

The closer you get to the middle of an artichoke head, the more succulent become the scales, until you reach the hairy immature flower bud, called the choke. Scrape the mass of hairs away with a spoon and you are left with a neck and stem that is exceedingly tender and the meatiest part of all.

Artichokes are usually grown from seeds or root divisions. Not all varieties grow quickly enough from seed to be practical, but 'Green Globe' gives you the best chance. Seeds should be started indoors 8 to 10 weeks before outdoor planting. Grow plants in peat pots indoors, then, after all danger of frost is past, transplant outside into a deeply worked, fertile soil, especially one high in phosphorus. Artichokes are heavy feeders, and they need lots of moisture to grow quickly. In 100 days the edible flower buds should start to appear. Northern gardeners should grow artichokes in a special cold frame, where plants can overwinter so they come back every year as perennials. The lid of the cold frame should be removed completely during summer so the huge, silver-blue leaves can grow large. Artichokes are such beautiful plants that you may even want to use them for ornamental foliage effects in flower beds.

In areas with mild winters, the largest specimens are assured if, in early spring, the crown is pruned of all but four main shoots. In the Northeast, space plants 3 feet (90cm) apart in rows 4 feet (1.2m) apart. In areas with mild winters, where plantings can perennialize, space plants 4 feet (1.2m) apart in rows 6 feet (1.8m) apart.

Artichoke,
Jerusalem

These bright yellow blooms and edible tubers are all from a single Jerusalem artichoke plant.

This native American perennial sunflower is an extremely aggressive root crop that will readily take over your entire vegetable plot if allowed free reign. A single tuber can increase fiftyfold in a single season, even in poor soil. The roots are hardy and will come back every year, growing tall, brittle stems topped with yellow, daisylike flowers in autumn.

Rather than give Jerusalem artichokes precious row space, prepare a special bed for them at the edges of your property, where they can be allowed to multiply without becoming invasive. Cover the tubers with 2 inches (5cm) of soil, spaced 2 feet (60cm) apart in rows spaced 4 feet (1.2m) apart. In autumn take a strong garden fork, raise the entire root system with its mass of tubers, and save one tuber from each clump to be your next season's crop.

Dug from the soil in autumn, Jerusalem artichokes store easily in a dark, cool, frost-free place.

A word of caution before you start substituting these tasty root vegetables for potatoes—they are high in insulin, a hormone that controls sugar in the body and is used to control diabetes. An intake of two or three tubers a week is normally fine, but too many can make you sick.

Arugula

Arugula is a hardy, fast-growing salad green with a pleasant nutty taste that is ideal for enlivening a mixed salad.

Also known as roquette or rocket, this rapid-growing spring green has ruffled leaves and a flavor reminiscent of watercress. Use it fresh in salads and sandwiches, or cooked in soups and as a nutritious side dish, just as you would use spinach or watercress.

Arugula is ready to eat just 45 days after sowing seeds directly into the garden, and plants are quite hardy. The seeds germinate at low temperatures and can be sown into the garden in early spring, as soon as the soil can be worked. Plant seeds ¼ inch (0.6cm) deep; when seedlings emerge thin them to stand 4 to 6 inches (10 to 15cm) apart in rows 2 feet (60cm) apart. Also, seeds can be scattered thickly to make a block of greens, since the plants tolerate crowding. To harvest, uproot entire plants or pick individual leaves as they mature.

Asparagus

Asparagus is a popular home-garden vegetable for several reasons—it is a hardy perennial that comes back year after year; it produces edible young stalks (called "spears") early in spring; and it is easy to grow. Until recently, the choice of varieties was limited, and about the only variety available to home gardeners was 'Mary Washington'. The old varieties produce two kinds of plants—males and females. Females bear red berries and generally are not as succulent or thick-stemmed as male plants, which are not weakened by going to seed.

About ten years ago I encountered a new kind of asparagus in the test plots at Pennsylvania State University. These were all-male hybrids that had been developed by Rutgers University in New Jersey, and also at a Dutch breeding establishment. Yield data showed the best of these were capable of yielding as much as three times more edible spears than the old nonhybrids.

Unfortunately, the best Rutgers variety, 'Jersey Giant', got a bad rap when it was first introduced because a production slip resulted in an unacceptable percentage of females. But no more! The crop has been thoroughly cleaned up, and in addition to 'Jersey Giant', which now offers 100 percent all-males, there are also 'Jersey Prince' and 'Jersey Knight'.

My own experience with these super males is that they grow faster from seedlings than they do from roots, although many mail order seed companies offer only the roots. I like to start the seeds early and have 8- to 12-week-old seedlings to transplant after frost-danger in spring. Once in the soil, the green, ferny fronds start collecting chlorophyll and quickly overcome transplant shock, while plants bought from roots are still sitting dormant in the soil. From seedlings I have been able to make a light harvest of spears the very next season.

/For best results, asparagus needs a well-drained, fertile, sandy-loam soil. When planting roots, place them 6 inches (15cm) deep, and leave the planting hole only half-filled with soil until green shoots emerge. The bed must be kept weed-free, so it is helpful to lay a covering of shredded leaves, grass clippings, or wood chips around the plants.

All-male asparagus hybrids produce up to three times more edible spears.

Well-rotted compost or stable manure worked into the topsoil is also beneficial. A high-phosphorus fertilizer like bone meal is excellent for strong root development. Space plants 3 feet (90cm) apart in rows spaced 3 feet (90cm) apart.

In areas where there is a lot of commercial asparagus production—like parts of New Jersey and California—the asparagus beetle can present a problem, but organic insect sprays like rotenone and pyrethrum will keep it under control. Much more important is ensuring excellent drainage by creating a raised planting bed. In France, where I have seen all-male asparagus grown from special clones not available to home gardeners, the asparagus spears may grow as thick as a man's wrist; more realistic for home gardeners are spears as thick as a man's thumb.

Beans,
Fava

The British call them broad beans—they have long, fat, pillowy pods, with a white, felt-like lining and large, green beans the size of limas, but thicker and meatier. These unusual beans turn gray on cooking, and tend to be an acquired taste. Many people have an allergic reaction to fava beans. Personally, I love them, and to be sure of a crop before hot weather finishes them off I erect temporary plastic tunnels over them in early spring, removing the plastic after danger of severe frosts. Though the plants themselves are extremely hardy, the flowers do not pollinate in extreme cold.

Plant the seeds 2 inches (5cm) deep, 6 inches (15cm) apart in rows spaced at least 3 feet (90cm) apart.

Fava beans are a magnet for black aphids, which colonize the lead shoots. Rub or blast them off with strong jets of water and keep disturbing them until they disappear.

The fava bean, or broad bean, is hardy and demands a combination of high soil fertility and cool growing conditions to mature its heavy crop of large, plump seeds. Unlike the pods of snap beans, however, those of fava beans are not edible. Plant the seeds as early in the spring as possible.

Beans,

Lima

When the 'Fordhook Lima' bean was first introduced by Burpee seeds in 1890, it was the world's first large-seed bush lima bean. Named for Burpee's Fordhook Farm, where its unique qualities were first recognized, the beans cost 75 cents for four seeds, and Burpee would not sell more than one packet per customer. In fact, the elder Mr. Burpee advised his customers not to eat them, but to use the four seeds as a seed crop, since he expected them to be scarce the next year, too! Since the introduction of the original 'Fordhook Lima', the USDA has introduced an improved disease-resistant type, 'Fordhook 242'.

There is now a large-seeded lima bean called 'Dr. Martin's', which is two to three times larger than the original 'Fordhook Lima', though not much larger than 'King of the Garden', a pole lima bean known for its extra-large seeds.

If you want something really different in lima beans, grow 'Fell's Scarlet Lima', a variety I have been nurturing for the past seven years. One vine of this pole lima will produce up to a thousand pods filled with three or four scarlet-red seeds. It's a late variety (100 days), and needs warm, fertile soil and full sun, but it's unmistakably different.

Lima beans should be planted directly into the garden after all danger of frost is past. Set the seeds 2 inches (5cm) deep, 6 inches (15cm) apart in rows spaced at least 4 feet (1.2m) apart. The seed is susceptible to rot from cold and poor drainage. In northern gardens consider pregerminating the seeds indoors in moist paper towels and planting them outside after all danger of frost. The pole varieties need strong supports—indeed, 'King of the Garden' will easily grow to a height of 30 feet (9.1m) in one season.

Serious pests are slugs and snails, which will attack and defoliate seedlings as soon as they emerge through the soil. Reduce the populations of these pests by hand picking in the early morning when they can be clearly seen.

Beans,
Shell

Alot of beans are grown for their seeds rather than their pods. 'Black Turtle' is a popular shell bean for making black bean soup. 'Vermont Cranberry' is a white bean speckled like a wren's egg, with the same coloring on its pods. See "Beans, Snap" for culture.

Above: This mixture of shell beans includes plain white navy beans as well as bicolored and speckled varieties, all of which can be dried for long storage. Right: 'Lazy Wife' heirloom pole snap beans have edible pods and are rated the most tender snap beans when cooked.

Beans,
Snap

All good snap beans prefer a continental climate, with lots of sunshine and warm soil, so I prefer them to the scarlet runners and French filets of European origin that do well in a maritime climate like England's (or San Francisco's), where plants are exposed to lots of rain or sea mists and cool summers.

There is one big advantage to pole beans—they will keep bearing all summer while the bush varieties give a quick flush of pods. Bush beans usually produce their pods within 55 days of sowing the seeds, so for a continuous supply of bush snaps you must make a succession of sowings 3 to 4 weeks apart until the end of August.

Plant seeds 1 inch (2.5cm) deep, 4 inches (10cm) apart in rows spaced at least 2 feet (60cm) apart, after all danger of frost.

The best of the bush snap beans are very good and they are now completely stringless (though a common term for them is still "string" beans). I particularly like 'Goldcrop', an All-America winner with yellow beans as straight as a pencil; 'Blue Lake', which bears luscious blue-green pods crowded fifty to a plant, and 'Romano II', an Italian romano type with flat pods and a supreme tenderness after cooking. Purple-podded 'Royal Burgundy' and giant 'Jumbo' (a cross between a romano and 'Kentucky Wonder') also win space at Cedaridge Farm most years for sheer good looks as well as good flavor. But the one snap bean I will never be without is a heritage variety, introduced nationally in 1888, called 'Lazy Wife,' a flavorful, stringless variety. At one time it was close to being lost from cultivation after most seed catalogs dropped it for earlier-maturing, more disease-resistant varieties.

Beans,

Soy

Soybeans were absent from North American seed catalogs until the Swedish soybean 'Fiskby V' was introduced. Before 'Fiskby V' the public knew soybeans only as oily, distasteful agricultural seeds grown by farmers for commercial purposes. Unfortunately, its popularity in England was short-lived owing to a series of cool summers, but it is alive and well in North America, and it deserves much wider recognition as a valuable food crop.

I must admit, though, that knowing how to shell and prepare edible soybeans is helpful. The pods are tough as shoe

The edible soybean 'Butterbean'—not to be confused with oily agricultural varieties—is sweet and delicious.

leather, and at the most there are three pea-sized beans to a pod, so it is tedious trying to shell enough beans to make a meal. It was Takeo Sakata, a Japanese seedsman, who showed me the easiest way to shell them for a snack. Just harvest a basket of pods by pulling the entire plant up by the roots and stripping it clean (the pods all mature at the same time). Then place the pods in some boiling salty water for about 10 minutes, drain, and let cool. When they're cool enough to handle, pick a pod between your thumb and forefinger, and squirt the beans into your mouth. They are delicious—

meaty and buttery in flavor. The boiling softens the skins so that a little pressure on one end will free the beans. Of course, if you prefer you may squirt them into a dish and eat them more elegantly with a fork, but I always grow them to eat as snacks while watching television or sunbathing on a hot summer's day.

In addition to 'Fiskby V', there is an excellent variety from Maine called 'Butterbean' and another from New Hampshire called 'Envy'. Edible soybeans are highly productive, and they grow bushy and compact. Just plant the seeds 1 inch (2.5cm) deep after all danger of frost, spacing plants 6 inches (15cm) apart in rows spaced at least 2 feet (60cm) apart.

The only problem I have ever encountered is with deer, which eat the plants even before the pods mature. Either fence the plot or cover plants with floating row covers.

Beets

When I first started in the seed industry there was one overriding favorite among beets—'Detroit Dark Red' (also called 'Redhart'). 'Detroit Dark Red' is still a top seller, but now home gardeners can grow white beets, golden beets, and even pink beets. To add a little more confusion there are also hybrid beets.

First, I must confess that I have an extremely strong bias towards 'Burpee's Golden Beet' (55 days). The golden roots are tender and delicious and do not bleed like red beets. They are excellent in salads and pickled, and the tops taste better

The pink tubers of 'Chioggia' show a distinct bull's-eye pattern when sliced.

than spinach when boiled as greens. The roots develop rapidly yet do not become fibrous or lose their sweet flavor when larger. They are at their best when eaten small.

Some interesting new beet developments have come along, including 'Formanova' and 'Cylindra'—both cylindrical beets shaped more like carrots—and 'Chioggia', a very appealing Italian beet that looks scarlet-red on the outside but, when sliced across the middle, shows concentric rings of rosy red and white. The greens are luscious and good to eat, and the roots are tender when cooked, especially if they are harvested when they are just a little larger than a golf ball.

Above left: 'Burpee's Golden Beet' sometimes experiences erratic germination, but the roots are tender and extremely tasty. The leaves are also edible, and make an excellent substitute for spinach. Above right: The 'Warrior' red beet is a popular hybrid that is extra tender and delicious when cooked.

Occasionally, you will see a white beet offered, but there is hardly any demand among home gardeners for white beets. However, hybrids, the latest development in beets, are definitely worth considering. 'Warrior' and 'Ace' are the two most widely available. They are extra early, disease-resistant and consistently tender.

The secret of good flavor in beets is rapid, unchecked growth through regular amounts of water and adequate spacing. Deprived of moisture, the roots can become deformed and fibrous, with conspicuous, hard rings. Crowding plants hampers growth and again leads to tough, fibrous, misshapen roots. It is extremely important not to disturb the roots. Also, cool temperatures produce the best yields, so time plantings for maturity in spring or fall. A sandy-loam soil is preferred.

In spring, sow seeds directly into the garden 4 weeks before the last expected frost date, since beet seedlings can tolerate mild frosts. However, be aware that in a packet of beet seeds the seeds will usually be in clusters unless the packet says "debearded seed" (meaning that the clusters have been separated into individual seeds). With clustered seeds, no matter how hard you try to space beets to avoid thinning you will always have little clumps springing up together, making some thinning essential. Plant the seeds a ½ inch (1.2cm) deep, and thin them to stand 3 to 4 inches (7 to 10cm) apart in the row, with at least 12 inches (30cm) between rows.

Since groundhogs, rabbits, and deer all like beet tops, fence these critters out. The only other serious problem is scab, a corky skin blemish that also affects potatoes. It is more prevalent in alkaline soil than acidic soils.

Broccoli

Even after the main head has been cut, many broccoli plants continue to produce smaller heads on sideshoots.

Only two broccoli varieties have won All-America Awards—both were bred in Japan. These are 'Green Comet', hybrid which is capable of maturing incredibly quickly (44 days from transplanting if it's watered regularly), and 'Premium Crop' hybrid (58 days), which is noted for its gigantic heads. When the main head of 'Green Comet' is cut additional sideshoots appear and extend the harvesting period. With 'Premium Crop' there are no sideshoots—all the plant's energy goes into producing one massive head that can measure up to 10 inches (25cm) across. The edible heads are actually tight clusters of immature buds. If not harvested when mature the buds unfold into a mass of yellow flowers, a process that is speeded up by hot weather.

In addition to the heading types, there is sprouting broccoli. Sprouting broccoli simply grows dozens of small heads on numerous sideshoots—the more you cut the more sprouts the plant produces, until hot weather exhausts it. When I lived in Scotland I used to see beautiful plantings of a broccoli called 'Romanesco', with bud clusters that formed an attractive spiral pattern like sea coral. Several North American seed catalogs feature it, but it is difficult to grow except in some cool, high-elevation and coastal areas.

Broccoli, like cauliflower, is a member of the cabbage family. All three can be started together 6 weeks before outdoor planting so you have a 5-inch (12.5cm) transplant. All are hardy and if hardened-off can be transferred to the garden several weeks before the last frost date—even earlier if protected by floating row covers or plastic tunnels. Plant seeds a ¼ (0.6cm) inch deep and space transplants 1½ feet (45cm) apart in rows spaced at least 2 feet (60cm) apart. Broccoli also makes an excellent fall crop when planted in late summer.

Heavy loam soils high in nitrogen—rather than loose, sandy soils—help form the tightest heads. Water whenever the soil surface feels dry and keep the soil cool by using a mulch of straw.

Broccoli's biggest problem is worms—actually a green caterpillar larva that hides below the bud clusters and eats the heads, causing discoloration. I once read a government nutritional analysis on broccoli and wondered why it showed a protein content. The answer was that the analysis was done on heads that had a few protein-rich worms hidden among them! To prevent serious damage from worms the bacterial control BT (*Bacillus thuringiensis*) is effective when used according to label directions. Also, for picture-perfect broccoli, consider covering young plants with floating row covers, which protect them from deer as well as insects.

Like all cabbage crops, broccoli needs cool nights to mature, along with a heavy fertile loam rather than sandy soil. Whenever there are three days without natural rainfall, water the plants.

Brussels Sprouts

Brussels sprouts are usually best grown as an autumn crop, since they require cool weather to flourish. Plan for a harvest to start after the first frost.

Though not an easy crop for many parts of North America, the rate of success is much improved when brussels sprouts are grown as a fall crop. Many varieties need 100 days to reach maturity, and they must have cool weather to make tall stems crowded with plump sprouts. Also, the flavor of the sprouts is much improved after exposure to a light frost.

The only brussels sprout to win an All-America award is 'Jade Cross' hybrid. It is early, high yielding, and the easiest of all brussels sprouts for home gardeners to grow. However, in recent years seed companies have switched from 'Jade Cross' to an improved version called 'Jade E'. It matures 5 days later, but it has longer stems, more sprouts, and tolerance to botrytis, a fungal disease.

Most sprouts have a bittersweet flavor from mustard oils and are an acquired taste, especially among children. In recent years the British have been working on strains that are low in mustard oils and therefore much sweeter. The earliest is 'Icarus' (100 days). Try an experimental planting before you decided to switch from the 'Jade' strains.

For a fall crop, start brussels sprouts 6 weeks before outdoor planting. For a fall crop in northern states delay the move to outdoors until the end of June. Transplants should be 4 to 5 inches (10 to 12cm) high. Mulch with straw to keep the soil cool and water whenever there are 3 days without rainfall. Keep a sharp eye out for colonies of aphids that will gather along the stem, causing dehydration. Blast these colonies off with jets of water or use floating row covers to lock them out.

Space plants 2 feet (60cm) apart in rows spaced 3 feet (90cm) apart. At time of frost, pinch out the tip so all the sprouts along the stem fatten up quickly. Brussels sprouts are extremely hardy and I have frequently trudged through snow to gather a harvest as late as Christmas.

Cabbage,
Chinese

There are two kinds of Chinese cabbage—a heading kind characterized by upright, oval heads and bright green leaves and bok choy, a nonheading type grown for its crisp, white ribs and dark green leaves. The heading type requires a longer growing season (usually 60 to 75 days from transplanting, depending on variety), while the nonheading types are extremely fast-growing (usually 45 days from seeding).

Both demand cool weather to mature, and may be grown as either a spring or fall crop. Planting is the same as for European cabbage, except bok choy varieties may be direct seeded. Plant seeds ¼ inch (0.6cm) deep and thin to stand 6 inches (15cm) apart in rows spaced 12 inches (30cm) apart.

Nonheading varieties of Chinese cabbage, such as bok choy, are much quicker and easier to grow than the heading types. Both kinds are hardy and prefer cool growing conditions. The crisp ribs and luscious green leaves of bok choy make a delectable side dish when cooked.

Cabbage,

E u r o p e a n

'Stonehead' cabbage, winner of an All-America Award, is a compact, disease-resistant variety.

Cabbage is a cool-weather vegetable grown as a winter crop in the South, and as a spring or fall crop in northern states. The original European cabbages brought to America by colonists have smooth, round heads; later, red-headed kinds were introduced; and then savoy types with blistered leaves and a reputation for the finest flavor were developed. Most home gardeners want one cabbage for earliness and another for large size to brag about around the neighborhood. The best early cabbage is 'Stonehead' hybrid (67 days) which is only 7 days later than 'Earliana' (60 days), the earliest-maturing cabbage. 'Stonehead' won an All-America Award for its disease resistance (especially to a common rot disease called yellows) and its extremely solid heads.

The cabbage I grow mostly for size is 'OS Cross' hybrid, an All-America winner that produces 20-pound cabbages in just 60 days. When I grow a red, it's always the All-America winner, 'Ruby Ball' hybrid; when I grow a savoy type its always the award-winning 'Savoy Ace' (80 days). Regular amounts of moisture and a straw mulch to keep the soil cool are essential for the biggest heads.

Start seeds 6 weeks before outdoor planting, sowing seeds ¼ inch (0.6cm) deep. Plants can be set into the garden several weeks before the last frost date if they are hardened-off. Space plants 2 feet (60cm) apart in rows 3 feet (90cm) apart. Plants prefer well-drained, high-nitrogen, heavy loam soils enriched with garden compost. The biggest pest is the cabbage white butterfly, which lays its egg clusters among the leaves. The eggs hatch, producing green caterpillars with voracious appetites. Control with BT—the bacterial disease that is harmless to humans—or cover maturing plants with floating row covers. Floating row covers will also protect cabbage crops against foraging animals like deer.

Cardoon

A close relative of the artichoke, cardoons grow much taller—up to 10 feet (3m) high in a season. The flower buds are not edible, but if the young stalks are bunched together with string in early spring and blanched like stalks of celery, the tender, lower-stem sections can be chopped into soups and stews for a celerylike consistency and flavor.

Like artichokes, cardoons are tender perennials that are killed by freezing. However, they do tolerate mild frosts, and in northern states a covering of plastic will often pull them through the winter. Cardoons are also suitable for growing as ornamental foliage highlights in mixed borders.

In its juvenile stage, the blanched stalks of the cardoon make a fine cooked vegetable; if left to mature, cardoons grow into gigantic thistles.

Carrots

H istorically, it is the French who have made the most significant advances in carrot breeding, and that is why the leading varieties have French names—'Danvers', 'Chantenay', and 'Nantes', for example. Remarkably, today's carrots are all descended from the weedy Queen's Ann's lace, a wildflower common throughout Europe and North America. The biggest breakthrough in recent years has been a series of hybrids, mostly from American and Dutch plant breeders. These hybrids are really "super carrots"—earlier, disease-resistant, more deeply colored, and more nutritious. Carrots with "Spartan" in their variety name, like 'Spartan Premium' (57 days to maturity), are products of an aggressive breeding program at Michigan State University.

It's fun to watch plant breeders evaluate carrots. They loosen the soil with a fork, then pull the roots out by hand and make notes on those that came up intact, without the stems breaking. Then they score for size, color, and flavor. Finally, they slice the carrot across the middle and measure the central core. Small cores score highest because that means an extra-tender carrot. For the home gardener, a top-shaped carrot like 'Short n' Sweet' is more desirable than one with an icicle shape because top-shaped carrots don't need as careful a soil preparation.

There's lots of interest nowadays in baby carrots because people love to eat them as healthy snacks. 'Minicor' (54 days) is a good Dutch strain, but forget 'Thumbelina', the most ridiculous carrot I've ever seen. It's round like a radish and it's the devil to peel. You need about four 'Thumbelinas' to make one 'Chantenay'. I grew it once out of curiosity—never again!

Carrot seed is tiny and it needs to be sown sparsely so that the seedlings can be thinned to stand at least 1 inch (2.5cm) apart, in rows spaced 12 inches (30cm) apart. Cover the seeds with only enough soil to anchor them. Take care that the soil does not form a crust after seeds are sown, since crusting of the soil inhibits germination. Sowing pelleted seed is helpful because a biodegradable clay coating around the seed makes handling easier and reduces the amount of thinning needed. Deep, sandy soils are best for carrots. If yours is shallow or clayey, it pays to prepare a special raised bed with sand and fine compost added (but avoid using coarse compost or coarse manure as this causes deformed roots).

The herb sage is a good companion plant for carrots, as it deters the carrot fly. Nematodes can cause deformed roots, and where soil is infested with nematodes the soil must be sterilized. Most carrot problems are associated with storage and the many rots that can occur. Studies have shown that the speed of curing prior to storage is critical. The more rapidly carrots are cooled to an ideal 32°F (0°C) storage temperature, the less rot develops. Also, more rot develops in carrots from poorly drained soils than in those grown in sandy soils with good drainage.

Mixed varieties of carrots portray a generous harvest. The roots of these carrots are perfectly formed and blemish-free because they were grown in raised beds of sandy soil that were sifted to remove foreign matter. Shallow, clay, or stony soils cause carrots to fork and split.

Cauliflower

There is an unusual orange cauliflower called 'Orange Bouquet' (75 days), which retains its color even after cooking, unlike purple cauliflower, which changes to green. Only one cauliflower has ever won an All-America Award. It is 'Snow Crown' hybrid (55 days), developed in Japan by the great Takii seed breeding concern, whose test gardens near Kyoto I have visited. 'Snow Crown' produces huge heads—up to 16 inches (40.6cm) across—though it is susceptible to a harmless pink discoloration caused by anthocynin disease. More recently Takii has introduced an improvement over 'Snow Crown' called 'Snow Grace' with snow-white curds, and only 3 days later in maturing. Both have extremely tight heads that produce a crisp, clean flavor whether eaten fresh or cooked.

Even cauliflower varieties that are noted for extra whiteness can be discolored by inclement weather, so consider folding the long jacket leaves up over the head and tying upright. If this sounds like too much work, there are some self-blanching types such as 'Avalanche' (75 days). Leaves of these self-blanching varieties automatically curl up over the head to protect it.

Planting of cauliflower is identical to broccoli, with the seeds starting indoors 6 weeks before outdoor planting. Plant the seed ¼ inch (0.6cm) deep and when transplants are 5 inches (12.5cm) high, transfer them to the garden after hardening-off. Space plants 2 feet (60cm) apart in

This handsome head of 'Snow Crown' cauliflower is ready for picking.

rows spaced 3 feet (90cm) apart. Mulch the base of plants with straw or another organic material. Time plantings so that maturity occurs either in late spring before summer heat or in autumn. Just be careful in spring not to set too large a plant into the garden before the last frost. With large plants, frost can cause the heads to bolt to seed. The same caterpillars that attack broccoli heads also attack cauliflower. Use BT bacterial control or floating row covers to eliminate them.

Rot diseases can also attack cauliflower, but these usually occur when gardeners do not practice crop rotation, winter cleanup, and annual soil improvement.

Celery

'Tall Utah' celeries have become the standard for excellence. The flavor of these green-stalked varieties is improved by blanching.

Celery is grown for its crisp, crunchy, edible leaf stalks that grow upright in a clump. It likes a fertile soil with plenty of compost or well-decomposed animal manure worked in and requires regular watering at all stages of development. Mulching the rows with straw will help to conserve moisture and keep the soil cool.

Most people like celery that is white, or "blanched," because of its appealing flavor when eaten fresh, but green celery has more nutritional value. There are several self-blanching kinds that fall somewhere between blanched and green varieties. These self-blanching types are creamy yellow or white towards the base of the stalk and green at the top. None of the self-blanching types, however, will produce a celery stalk as clean and white as when the stalks of a green celery plant are blanched. Blanch celery stalks by fitting them with a brown paper collar when they start to mature, or pile shredded leaves or soil against the stalks up to the crown of leaves.

Celery is best started indoors 6 weeks before you intend to plant it outdoors. Plant seeds ¼ inch (0.6cm) deep. About 3 weeks after danger of frost, transfer the seedlings to the garden to stand 12 inches (30cm) apart in rows spaced 2 feet (60cm) apart. 'Tall

Utah 52-70 Improved' (110 days) is a top-quality green-stalked variety that can be blanched white. 'Stokes Golden Plume' (90 days) is one of the few self-blanching types still offered today.

Chard,
Swiss

Tomatoes and beans have been the most popular home garden vegetables for generations. Out of fifty types of

Colorful 'Rainbow' chard was developed by New Zealand seedsman John Eaton using pollen from various types of beets.

home garden vegetables, Swiss chard is probably number twenty-five in popularity. All that is likely to change when enough people have tried a new variety of multicolored Swiss chard called 'Rainbow'. It is without doubt the most colorful vegetable you could wish to grow, with stalks that are not only white and red, but also cream, lemon, deep yellow, orange, apricot, rosy red, pink, and striped! And it is more tender than the white or red varieties that have been around for decades. Indeed, it now makes old, established varieties like 'Ruby' (red) and 'Lucullus' (white) almost obsolete.

Chard is closely related to beets, and the seeds, which are clustered together in threes and fours, even look like beet seeds. Consequently, when you sow the seeds you generally have several sprouts from each cluster, making thinning essential. Chard can be direct-sown several weeks before the last frost date in your area, as it will tolerate even severe frosts, but with 'Rainbow' chard it is better to start seed indoors in a seed tray so that you can separate the best colors for transplanting to the garden. You can even create a patchwork design by planting all the orange varieties in one block, all the red in another, and all the yellow in another.

Plant the seed a ½ inch (1.2cm) deep and thin seedlings to stand at least 12 inches (30cm) apart in rows spaced at least 2 feet (60cm) apart. They are fast-growing and will be ready for harvesting in 60 days. Since deer and other foraging animals can eat an entire planting of chard to the ground in one go, fence animals out wherever they present a problem. Apart from that, chard is extremely easy to grow and by harvesting the outer leaves you can maintain a planting all season. Chard will last even into winter months, as the plants are hardy biennials that are only finished off by a hard freeze.

The red and multicolored 'Rainbow' chards are not only suitable for jazzing up the vegetable garden, they can be used ornamentally in container plantings and flower beds. At the famous French garden of Villandry, where vegetables are planted for ornamental effect in a vast parterre garden, chard is used extensively.

Cook chard leaves as you would spinach and chop the ribs up like celery. The ribs are especially delicious when braised and sprinkled with bread crumbs or added to soups as a substitute for bok choy. The leaves and ribs also freeze well.

For good flavor in radicchio, a cool growing season and plenty of water are essential. 'Guilio', shown here, is a red-leafed, heading radicchio variety.

Chicory, Endive, *and* Radicchio

There are three kinds of chicory: a forcing type used to produce "chicons" (also known as Belgian endive); a leaf type called endive that produces either loose or firm heads, depending on the variety; and a heading type that produces red leaves called radicchio.

Chicons are immature leaves that form a sheath above a root when the root is first held in the dark, then exposed to warmer temperatures. Forcing chicory is challenging to grow unless you have a place to store deep boxes filled with a peat-based potting soil. The roots for forcing are lifted from the garden in fall and placed in the deep boxes with the crowns at the soil surface. A 5-inch (12.5cm) layer of straw or shredded leaves is placed over the crowns for the chicons to grow into when the soil temperature is raised to between 40° and 50°F (4° and 10°C). 'Flash', developed by a French breeding station, takes 110 days to grow mature roots suitable for forcing.

Leaf-type chicories form beautiful rosettes of succulent green leaves like lettuce. The favored variety for North America is 'Sugarhat'. If the leaves are not harvested and the plant is allowed to go to seed, it produces beautiful, sky blue, daisylike flowers that are similar to wild chicory. The roots of chicory have a flavor like coffee and can be ground to make a coffee substitute.

Leaf-type chicory is grown like lettuce, with seeds sown directly into the garden several weeks before the last frost date. Sow the seeds ¼ inch (0.6cm) deep, and thin the seedlings to stand 12 inches (30cm) apart in rows spaced 2 feet (60cm) apart.

Endive is closely related to chicory. A favorite variety is 'Green Curled' (42 days). Direct seeding must occur several weeks before the last frost date (or in late summer) for plants to mature during cool weather. Otherwise, seeding and spacing is the same as for leaf-type chicory.

Radicchio is a prized salad vegetable because of its intense ruby coloring. Most varieties are a challenge to grow, as they need cool conditions and regular watering in order to form their rounded heads of tightly folded leaves and bittersweet flavor. 'Guilio'(60 days) is the only variety I have had success with, grown as a spring crop.

Sow seeds ¼ inch (0.6cm) deep, and space seedlings to 8 inches (20cm) apart in rows 18 inches (45cm) apart.

Chicory, endive, and radicchio all need protection from slugs and snails. Remove these pests by hand in the early morning when their silvery trails show where they are feeding or hiding. Wood ashes scattered around plantings will also deter slugs and snails from crossing.

Above: Chicons are grown from chicory roots, which are forced under cover and in darkness to produce bittersweet, plump, creamy white leaf buds. The scoop-shaped, crispy leaves are good for dipping. Right: Curly endive bears a strong resemblance to lettuce.

Corn

Tremendous strides in breeding corns have been made in recent years, with super sweetness as the objective. It used to be that to ensure sweetness, you had to have the water boiling before picking the cobs, because standard varieties lose their flavor quickly once they are harvested. This no longer applies, and for superb sweet corn, just four words are enough to open and close the subject: 'How Sweet It Is'. This early white sweet corn was introduced by Twilley Seeds, and it won an All-America Award for its excellence. Not only is it super-sweet, it retains its sweetness for up to 10 days if stored in the vegetable bin of your re-frigerator. To ensure its excellent sweetness, isolate 'How Sweet It Is' from other sweet corns, as any cross pollination may reduce the quality. If you cannot find 'How Sweet It Is', try 'Honey and Pearls', a bicolored All-America winner. Of course, the variety that seems to have the best reputation is 'Silver Queen', a late variety (94 days) that does not need isolating to retain its sweetness. I used to grow 'Silver Queen' religiously, but it has weak brace roots, and after several seasons in which wind storms flattened the stalks and caused poorly formed ears, I have switched to 'Platinum Lady', which matures 14 days earlier.

Like all warm-season crops, sweet corn will benefit from a covering of plastic mulch over the soil to deter weeds and maintain a warm soil temperature. A well-drained, high-nitrogen soil in full sun is preferred. Also, it's best to plant sweet corn in blocks so that the tassels on top thoroughly pollinate the silks halfway down the plant. Only after pollination will the silks stimulate the cob to grow. For well-filled ears, sweet corn also needs plenty of water at the time of tasseling. In the absence of natural rainfall, irrigate the plants well.

Sometimes sweet corn can become infected with a black sooty mold that distorts the cobs. I once watched a Mexican friend harvest these diseased cobs and carefully scrape the black soot into a bowl. The next morning she served it to me for breakfast, mixed into scrambled eggs, and it tasted delicious—like mushrooms. When I voiced

astonishment she pulled a can off the shelf and showed me how I could purchase cans of the sooty mold in gourmet food stores!

Ornamental corns (which are not edible, but are grown purely for their beautiful exotic colors) and pop corns (which can be an assortment of colors, including white, yellow, black, red, and combinations thereof) need a longer growing season than most sweet corns (usually 100 days), but otherwise growing techniques are the same.

The 'Rainbow' variety of ornamental corn is grown mostly for decoration.

Cucumbers

There are seed catalogs that list forty-five varieties of cucumbers with bewildering classifications—slicing and pickle types and vining and bush are easy enough to understand, but what about black-spine and white-spine, self-fertile and all-female, indoor and outdoor, burpless and nonburpless, and other designations?

Most home gardeners want a fairly compact, disease-resistant, slicing variety, and any of the 'Marketmore' strain (such as 'Marketmore 76' [58 days]) fit this description. Every few years Dr. Henry Munger, who developed 'Marketmore' at Cornell University in New York, releases an updated version, usually with extra disease resistance. The sensational disease resistance of the 'Marketmore' strain is important, since wilt, mildew, and rot diseases are the most common cause of failure.

For containers and small spaces there are bush varieties, but these never yield as heavily as the vine types. To save space, vining kinds can be grown on a trellis, for cucumbers have tendrils that allow them to climb unaided. "All-female" means that there is a significantly larger number of female flowers than male ones, and "self-fertile" refers to varieties in which the females don't need cross-pollination, but these varieties are more for the commercial grower than the home gardener. Indoor cucumbers are specially bred for growing under glass (another consideration for commercial growers), while "burpless" and "nonburpless" refers to the bitterness that is absent in the skin of certain varieties. "Black spine" and "white spine" refers to the color of the tiny spines that develop along a cucumber fruit—this is nothing for home gardeners to be concerned about.

Sow seeds ½ inch (1.2cm) deep directly into the garden after all danger of frost. Group three seeds to each planting station and thin to one strong vine. Planting stations can be 2 feet (60cm) apart in rows spaced 4 feet (1.2m) apart. Allow the vines to spread into each other and knit together.

Striped cucumber beetles are a prime cause of disease; reduce their populations by growing cucumber vines under floating row covers or start spraying the vines early with a rotenone/pyrethrum organic insecticide.

For good yields of cucumbers, it's essential to plant disease-resistant varieties such as the 'Marketmore' strain.

To maintain a healthy vine, keep the vines picked. If you allow cucumber fruits to turn yellow, the vines quickly exhaust themselves.

Eggplant

When a particular variety dominates a class of vegetables there's little point in beating about the bush. The American-bred 'Dusky' hybrid is the perfect home garden variety. It is incredibly early (63 days), highly productive, and just the right size (6 to 7 inches [15cm to 17.5cm] long), with flawless, black, oval fruits. I well remember Ted Torrey, an eggplant breeder, telling me that when he first grew 'Dusky'—from a competitive breeder—he nearly gave up breeding eggplants because he simply could not see any way to improve upon it.

There is one serious problem with all eggplants. They are extremely attractive to flea beetles, which are about the size of a pin head and tend to colonize the underside of the leaves. When the plant's leaves look like they have been shot through with buckshot, they've fallen victim to flea beetles. The thousands of tiny holes cause the leaves to turn brown, and the plant dies. Flea beetles hate marigold foliage, and I have seen crops of eggplants protected by a companion planting of marigolds. Also, the organic pesticide combination pyrethrum/rotenone is effective.

I cannot understand the tendency among many seed houses to offer smaller and smaller eggplants, like 'Bambino' and 'Slim Jim'. They are thick-skinned, tough to peel, and difficult to cut into sticks for cooking. If you want something a little different in eggplants, grow the pink and white striped variety 'Rosa Bianca', which is beautiful in vegetable arrangements. Also, keep an eye open for the amazing 'Jordanian Tree' eggplant. Provide a mulch of black plastic and watch it soar into a small tree, branching

freely. It looks especially interesting grown in a tub, since it grows to the height of a human in a single season. The glossy black fruits are shaped like a purse, flared at the base, and slightly ribbed. I have grown up to fifty fruits on a single plant by starting the seed early indoors (8 weeks before outdoor planting) and transplanting after danger of frost into fertile soil.

Eggplants tolerate heat and humidity, but do need watering whenever there is a week without an inch of rainfall. The seeds resemble tomato seeds (the two plants are closely related) and need to be planted just ⅛ inch (0.3cm) deep. Space transplants 3 feet (90cm) apart in rows spaced 4 feet (1.2m) apart. Plants fare best when grown in wire cylinders 3 feet (90cm) high, so the side branches can be self-supporting, otherwise the ripening fruit can be so heavy that it breaks the branches.

Eggplants are a magnet for flea beetles; the holes in these leaves—scattered like buckshot—are evidence of their presence. Left unchecked, flea beetles are likely to bring an early end to this plant, a variety called 'Dusky' hybrid, which is otherwise the leading variety for earliness, good shape, and heavy yield.

Kale, Collards, *and* Mustard Greens

Kale, collards, and mustard greens are hardy leaf crops related to cabbage, grown for their edible leaves, which taste sweet after exposure to frost. Collards are a little later in maturing, and are more popular among southern gardeners. Mustard greens have a more piquant flavor. All will tolerate freezing temperatures and stand in the garden all winter, even when covered with snow. The most popular home garden kales are all curly-leaf types like 'Green Curled Scotch' (55 days). Plants can be grown as a spring crop or as a fall and winter crop.

Start seeds of both indoors 6 weeks before outdoor planting. Set transplants 1½ feet (45cm) apart in rows spaced 2½ feet (75cm) apart. To harvest, pick the outer leaves. This way, more new leaves will grow from the crown to keep the plants productive over a long period. They are best eaten lightly boiled or steamed as a side dish.

Curly kale (above right) and collards (right) are both members of the cabbage family, and are valued for their hardiness. These two vegetables provide a source of fresh cooked greens when the rest of the garden is dormant or harvested. 'Giant Red' mustard greens (above) display unusual bronze foliage.

Kohlrabi

A big benefit of this little-used vegetable is its rapid growth and early maturity. Related to cabbage, kohlrabi is mainly grown for the bulbous part of the stem, which tastes like a turnip when peeled and cooked.

There are two basic kinds of kohlrabi—white and purple—but the best variety to grow is 'Grand Duke' (45 days), because nothing else can beat it for earliness, size, and resistance to black rot disease. Developed in Japan, 'Grand Duke' won an All-America Award for its quality. The only problems I have encountered are with slugs scarring the skin and with splitting of the bulbs if they are not harvested early enough.

Seeds should be direct-sown into the garden several weeks before the last frost date, covered with ⅛ inch (0.3cm) of fine soil. Space plants at least 4 inches (10cm) apart in rows spaced 12 inches (30cm) apart. Plant again at the end of summer for a fall crop since kohlrabi likes cool temperatures.

Above: Though most varieties of kohlrabi are white, this variety has a purple skin and white interior. At this stage of maturity, the crisp flesh is tender and delicious when cooked. Left: For succulent, white stems like these, heap mulch around the base of 'Titan' leeks to exclude light.

Leeks

Leeks are part of an elite group of hardy vegetables that will stay in the garden well into the winter months, until they are literally frozen into the ground. Though they need a fairly long growing season to mature (100 days), they are easy to grow and have a wonderful, mild, oniony flavor. Cock-a-Leeky soup is a famous Scottish dish traditionally served hot during winter in front of a roaring log fire. Leeks are also good to eat as a side dish, simply boiled or steamed for a few minutes.

Leeks like fertile soil—either sandy or clay-based—with plenty of garden compost or well-decomposed animal manure mixed in. They also prefer soil with a high phosphorus content. Seeds may be started indoors 5 weeks before outdoor planting to produce seedling transplants or may be direct-sown into the garden, where they should be covered with ¼ inch (0.6cm) of soil. Thin plants to stand 2 inches (5cm) apart in rows 12 inches (30cm) apart. Plants tolerate mild frosts if hardened-off, and so for earliest yields should be placed outdoors several weeks before the last frost date.

The varieties 'Titan' and 'Giant Musselburg' (120 days) grow the fattest, most succulent stems. Soil grubs like wireworms can scar the stalks; for blemish-free stalks protect with a rotenone/pyrethum spray. The more white stem section the better, so it is advisable to start piling loose soil or shredded leaves against the stalks 4 to 6 weeks before harvesting.

Lettuce

Though looseleaf lettuces such as 'Sangria' (middle row) will tolerate crowding, heading varieties like 'Iceberg' (bottom row) need adequate spacing to develop tight, crispy heads.

The biggest myth about lettuce is that European varieties are best. In fact, the American 'Buttercrunch' is a superior variety with a crisp, buttery yellow heart. Another myth surrounds 'Iceberg' lettuce. Burpee introduced 'Iceberg' in 1894, and it was an instant success due to its tight, crisp, green outer leaves, its crisp, pale yellow center, and its long keeping quality. Burpee still sells its original 'Iceberg', but today it is confused with different strains of hard-headed lettuces specially grown for supermarkets. Many of these supermarket lettuces hold up well during shipment, but offer poor flavor and low nutritional value compared with the original.

Another misnomer involves Kentucky limestone lettuce. It's not a variety name but rather an appealing description for bibb lettuces like 'Buttercrunch' and 'Boston Bibb' grown on limestone soil. You can ensure a similar flavor sensation by growing 'Buttercrunch' or 'Boston Bibb' in soil that has been limed to sweeten it.

To ensure good quality with head lettuce spacing is vital. Give varieties like 'Buttercrunch' at least 8-inch (20cm) spacing in rows 2 feet (60cm) apart. Also, consider starting some seeds indoors for transplanting. Head lettuces take up to 60 days to mature, so transplanting seedlings can save up to 14 days.

The easiest lettuce to grow is leaf lettuce. It forms a loose rosette of leaves rather than a head, and it is fast-growing: varieties like 'Oakleaf' and 'Red Sails' mature in 50 days. It's possible to pick leaves from the outside of rosettes so you don't have to uproot whole plants. Sow seeds directly into the garden and cover with just enough soil to anchor them, as lettuce seeds like exposure to light to germinate. Plants can be thinned to stand 6 inches (15cm) apart in rows spaced 12 inches (30cm) apart, though leaf lettuce will tolerate crowding.

Another easy-to-grow lettuce is romaine, or cos. It doesn't form a head either, but holds its leaves up stiffly to form a sort of cocoon. The leaves have prominent, crisp mid-ribs and this type of lettuce is used most often for making Caesar salad. Most romaine lettuce grows tall—up to 2 feet (60cm) high—and needs spacing 8 to 12 inches (20 to 30cm) apart, but 'Little Gem' is a miniature romaine sufficient for serving two people. It tolerates crowding—even 4-inch (10cm) spacing—and it is the sweetest of all the romaine types.

The biggest problems with lettuce are slugs and snails. They will crawl right into the heart of a lettuce and eat leaf ribs, causing ugly brown streaks and a bitter flavor. Reduce populations by hand picking them off plants, or use floating row covers over rows of lettuce to create a barrier against the pests.

Above all, ensure that lettuce receives plenty of moisture. Hot, dry conditions cause the plants to bolt to seed. Sow again after midsummer so the plants can mature during cooler autumn weather. Also consider frost-extenders—such as floating row covers—to maintain your lettuce plantings even into winter months.

Melons

Cantaloupe and watermelon help to enliven a display of nutritious summer vegetables that includes tomatoes and squashes.

Melons are not easy to grow. They are easy to start, for they germinate rapidly started indoors, or direct-seeded into the garden after danger of frost, but they need full sun and room for the vines to spread. The soil must drain well (sandy soil preferable), and it must be fertile, preferably enriched with well-decomposed animal manure or garden compost. Melons—whether watermelons or cantaloupes—like to grow fast; they need water on a regular basis, but too much water, such as too much natural rainfall at time of ripening, can cause an insipid flavor.

Left: 'Yellow Baby' watermelon is almost seedless. Below: 'Star Headliner' cantaloupe is a delicious muskmelon variety.

Sow several seeds ½ inch (1.2cm) deep in clusters spaced at least 4 feet (1.2m) apart, after frost danger. Thin the seedlings to one vigorous plant in each cluster, and allow the vines to knit together as they grow.

It helps to cover the soil with black plastic, not only to suffocate weeds, but also to maintain a stable, above-average soil temperature, since the vines will stop growing when cool nights chill the roots. Above all, protect the vines from damage

by cucumber beetles—yellow and black striped bugs that chew the vine and introduce wilt diseases. Periodic sprays after transplanting, using an organic insecticide such as pyrethrum or rotenone will help control the beetle. Alternatively, the vines can be covered with a light horticultural fabric, such as Reemay, which lays over the plants like a spider's web, blocking entry of insects. Research has also shown that in short-season areas like Vermont and Maine, covering the soil with clear plastic is even more beneficial than black plastic because it heats the soil more quickly and maintains a warm soil temperature longer, allowing melons to mature earlier.

Choosing the correct variety is essential. Among watermelons I still favor 'Yellow Baby', not only because of its sweet flavor, cold tolerance, and almost seedless quality, but because it is usually the earliest to ripen and the vines stay productive into late summer, longer than other melons. At Cedaridge Farm visitors clamor for a taste of 'Yellow Baby'. The first fruits are usually ready for picking at the beginning of August.

Among cantaloupes I prefer either 'Burpee Hybrid' or 'Star Headliner', a variety from Twilley Seeds of Trevose, which is grown by more Amish farmers than any other variety. Both varieties produce large, heavily netted, deeply ribbed melons with an attractive beige skin. The inside is deep orange, juicy, and delicious. However, I think nothing among melons beats a well-grown Crenshaw, with fruits weighing up to 20 pounds each. They are oval in shape and have a yellowish glow when ripe; the center is a pale orange. Normally, Crenshaws need a long growing season, but one variety—Burpee's 'Early Hybrid Crenshaw'—will succeed in northern states. In New York restaurants you will pay $2.50 for a single slice of this wonderful fruit.

Some seed catalogs have made a big deal over the 'Charentais' melons that are grown in Spain and the south of France. They are small with a fruity perfume that permeates the skin, but for my money nothing can compete with a good old American cantaloupe like 'Burpee Hybrid', 'Gold Star', or 'Star Headliner'.

Okra

Okra's tender pods are best harvested when young; otherwise, they tend to become fibrous. Here you can see the unique shape of the pod when sliced as well as the slender whole pods.

Also called gumbo and lady's fingers, okra is related to hibiscus, and was brought to America from Africa by slave traders. In the South plants grow much taller than in the North—up to 6 feet (1.8m) high in one season. The bullet-hard seeds are best started indoors in a moist paper towel. As soon as the seed coats split, transfer the seeds to the garden after all danger of frost, planting ½ inch (1.2cm) deep, 1½ feet (45cm) apart.

Plants grow quickly during warm weather, producing white, hibiscuslike flowers that last only a day. When they drop they leave a green, horn-shaped seedpod, best picked when it is no more than 2 to 3 inches (5 to 7.5cm) long. It is exceedingly tender and succulent when young; as the pods age they quickly become fibrous and woody.

The ribbed pods can be cooked whole or sliced across to form a "Star of David" shape for adding to soups and stews. 'Annie Oakley' (52 days) is extra early, free of spines along the stems, and retains its tenderness longer than other okra varieties.

Onions

aturity in onions is governed by day length. An onion that does well in the South is unlikely to do well in the north, and vice versa. For example, the standard for quality among onions is a southern variety, 'Vidalia'. Unfortunately, even in the South it can be grown only in two counties of Georgia, where soil and climate combine to produce its mild flavor and large size. A more widely adapted southern onion is the 'Granex' strain. For northern states the 'Giant Walla Walla' onion (125 days) from Washington state almost matches 'Vidalia'. The British 'Ailsa Craig Exhibition' (110 days) is also a good 'Vidalia' substitute for northern conditions.

Since onion maturity times are from seed, start seeds 6 weeks before outdoor planting and transplant seedlings several weeks before the last frost date in your area. Plant seeds ¼ inch (0.6cm) deep. Onions are also grown from sets (small bulbs), though sets do not grow as high a quality onion as seedlings because the bulbs put a lot of energy into growing a seed stalk. Space sets or seedlings 3 inches (7.5cm) apart in rows spaced 18 inches (45cm) apart.

In mild winter areas, some onions (like 'Giant Walla Walla') are planted from seedlings in autumn, overwintered, and harvested at the end of summer. This timetable ensures the largest bulbs, but even from a spring planting in northern regions, 'Giant Walla Walla' is an excellent onion.

'Ailsa Craig Exhibition' is a large, white-fleshed, yellow-skinned onion suitable for cooler climates.

Onions like soils that are loaded with well-decomposed animal manure or garden compost and phosphorus. Also, the biggest bulbs are grown from raised beds covered with black plastic and watered almost daily.

Mild onions don't store as well as pungent onions. The best storage onions of all are called "sleeper" onions, like 'Spartan Sleeper' (120 days) and 'First Edition' (110 days), both for northern gardens. Stored even at room temperature the bulbs will remain crisp and usable for up to 9 months.

Parsnips

Parsnips, such as this 'Lancer' variety, need a sandy, screened, fertile soil in order to grow blemish-free roots.

Before carrots were developed as a root crop by the French, and before Sir Walter Raleigh introduced the potato into Europe from South America, parsnips were the most popular vegetable grown in European gardens. The roots can be stored for long periods of time, and thus enabled people to survive harsh winters. Parsnips take longer to grow than carrots, but they are more sweetly flavored when cooked, especially when mashed like potatoes, and the seeds are easier to handle.

Sow seeds directly into the garden several weeks before the last frost date and cover with ¼ inch (0.6cm) of soil. Thin seedlings to stand 4 inches (10cm) apart in rows spaced 1½ feet (45cm) apart. To hasten germination (which can take 21 days outdoors) consider pre-germinating the seed indoors in a moist paper towel. Since the roots can extend to 10 inches (25cm) deep and are easily deformed by obstructions, it's worth preparing a special raised bed with good drainage. If your soil is heavy mix it with sand and compost to promote drainage.

Harvest the roots in the fall after frost has helped to improve their flavor. Sink a garden fork into the ground and lever up the soil around the roots so they pull free easily without breaking. To store, remove the tops and place the roots side-by-side but not touching in a box filled with moist sand. Keep the box in a cool, dark place.

The British have never lost their liking for parsnips, and they continue to make progress in developing new varieties. 'Harris Model' used to be the best for North American conditions, but now 'Lancer' (120 days) represents an improvement, with smooth roots, sweet flavor, and canker resistance.

Peas,

Black-Eyed

Black-eyed peas are a favorite southern vegetable, since they are tolerant of heat and drought. Though they are legumes, like English peas, they are more closely related to beans, and must be cooked to be edible. The pods are slim and up to 6 inches (16cm) long, and may be either straight or curved. They can be green or purple at maturity, depending on the variety. The seeds themselves are usually white with black and pink "eyes."

Direct-sow seeds after all danger of frost, covering with 1 inch (2.5cm) of soil. Space seeds 6 inches (15cm) apart in rows spaced 3 feet (90cm) apart. Harvest the inedible pods when they turn brittle, and shuck the seeds onto burlap to dry thoroughly. Store the dried seeds in glass jars or cloth bags until ready to use. Black-eyed peas are delicious either boiled as a side dish or added to soups and stews. Plants are fast-growing during hot, humid weather, and can be ready for harvesting within just 50 days!

Two popular varieties are 'California Black-Eyed' and 'Pinkeye Purple Hull'.

Left: 'Pinkeye Purple Hull' is an extremely productive variety of black-eyed peas that can take the heat. The pods are not edible and turn brittle when mature. Below: 'Oregon Giant' pea pods are best eaten before the peas swell the pods.

Peas,

English

Each year I grow 'Green Arrow' (known today in Europe as 'Green Shaft'), a shelling pea with dark green, straight pods and up to twelve peas per pod; 'Knight', the most disease-resistant of early peas; and 'Sugar Snap', an edible-pod pea. These three varieties are all I will ever need for sensational yields and the finest flavor in peas. 'Sugar Snap' is a tall vining pea that needs strong supports to climb. Don't let that put you off—the dense foliage and long vines help produce its superb flavor and high yields. 'Green Arrow' grows to about 3 feet (90cm) high and can be self-supporting but I prefer to give it some netting for support, as this keeps the handsome peas clear off the ground. 'Knight' is a true dwarf, just 2 feet (60cm) high, and like 'Green Arrow' it can be self-supporting. It is resistant to pea wilt, several mosaic diseases, and powdery mildew. Its powdery mildew resistance is so good it is the only pea I can recommend for a fall harvest, when mildew kills most other pea varieties.

'Sugar Snap' differs from regular edible-podded peas (called snow peas) because snow peas (like 'Mammoth Melting Sugar' and 'Oregon Giant') must be harvested while the pods are flat and before the peas begin to swell the pod and turn bitter. 'Sugar Snap' peas can be eaten immature, when flat, but as the peas swell the pods both pods and peas become crisper and tastier until the pods actually turn pale and dry out. The fat, green pods may be eaten fresh off the vine. Just remove the stem section, which is attached to a suture (string) running the length of the pod. Pinching off the stem automatically removes the string.

Peas demand cool conditions and regular amounts of moisture. They will tolerate mild frosts and are best direct-sown into furrows 1 inch (2.5cm) deep, the plants thinned to 4 inches (10cm) apart, in rows at least 3 feet (90cm) apart. Soil should be fertile (especially high in nitrogen), well drained, and mulched to

'Sugar Snap' peas grow tasty, edible pods that can be harvested at any stage of development.

conserve soil moisture. As the season advances and days turn hot and humid, the vines will shrivel and die. As soon as production ceases, uproot the plants and discard them

'Sugar Snap' snap pea won an All-America Award for its plump, sweet, edible pods.

on your compost pile, planting the space with a fast-growing warm-season crop such as cucumbers or zucchini squash.

Peas are legumes that manufacture nitrogen through the development of nodules among their roots. Yields are considerably increased by dusting the seeds with inoculent—a black powder containing beneficial soil bacteria—before planting. The beneficial soil bacteria manufacture a stable source of nitrogen for peas.

Peppers,
Sweet and Hot

To grow a garden full of peppers you will need to start seeds indoors 6 to 8 weeks before outdoor planting. Of course, you can also wait until after danger of frost is past and buy transplants from a garden center, but you'll find the choice rather limited. After tomatoes I think peppers are probably my favorite vegetable.

Basically, peppers can be divided into sweet and hot varieties, but after that distinction there is tremendous choice in terms of color and shape. Take sweet bell peppers as an example: the most common color for the fruit is green, but most green peppers will turn red when fully mature. I also grow bell peppers that turn yellow, orange, choco-

late-colored, purple, or black. Chopped and mixed together, these peppers can make any salad extraordinarily
appealing. All can be eaten fresh off the vine like an apple,
chopped into salads, or cooked. They are delicious lightly

'Jingle Bells' is a highly productive, ever-bearing, early-fruiting sweet bell pepper that tolerates cool growing conditions.

steamed or roasted, especially when garnished with chopped-up pieces of coriander
(also known as Chinese parsley and cilantro).

For sheer size choose 'Big Bertha' or 'Gedeon' hybrid. They both produce extra-
large fruits that grow up to 10 inches (25cm) long and 5 inches (12.5cm) wide. There
is also a large-fruited, yellow variety called 'Golden Goliath' of similar proportions. Of
course, I also grow standard-size peppers because they are more productive than the
giants. I think the standard for excellence now is 'Bell Boy' hybrid, which won an All-
America Award for its productivity, extra-thick wells, blocky shape, and extraordinary
disease resistance.

Some years in northern gardens peppers get off to a slow start. If it rains a lot or
stays cool, most peppers stop growing, so for insurance I always include a planting of
'Gypsy' hybrid, a special cold-tolerant pepper that produces lemon yellow peppers that
turn red when mature. It is more elongated than your standard bell pepper, but is capable of setting a lot of fruit under adverse conditions.

I also grow a few hot peppers, such as red 'Cayenne' (very hot and shaped like a
slender icicle), 'Jalapeno' (a medium-hot cone-shaped pepper that is mostly harvested
when green since the summer season in northern gardens sometimes is not long enough
to turn them red) and 'Anaheim' (a long, tapering green pepper shaped like a scabbard

that turns red at maturity). 'Anaheim' is a mildly hot pepper, and I like to eat it stuffed with chopped onion, sliced cheese, and cubed tomato and heated just enough to melt the cheese.

Apart from the 'Anaheim', I don't actually eat many hot peppers, but I do find them useful for decoration. Red 'Cayenne' dries to a glossy red, and since the plants cover themselves in hundreds of fruits, the entire plant can be picked to hang as a Thanksgiving decoration.

There is a sweet bell pepper that I like to grow for ornamental effect. Called 'Jingle Bells', it produces up to fifty peppers on a plant, quickly turning scarlet-red and remaining that color for a long time. They are only about a third of the size of regular bell peppers, but the effect of so many ripe red fruits on a small bushy plant is quite extraordinary. To eat them, simply slice across the stem section, scoop the seeds out, and stuff the pepper with dip.

Peppers like a fertile soil with a high phosphorus content and good drainage. Phosphorus is a plant nutrient that stimulates flower formation and fruit ripening. If your soil is overly acidic, add lime. A little lime in combination with regular watering will also help prevent a common pepper disease called blossom-end rot, which can also affect tomatoes. Telltale symptoms are black patches at the fruit tips that eventually cause the entire fruit to rot. Peppers are also susceptible to sunscald, which occurs when the fruits are exposed to the direct rays of the sun without partial shade from foliage.

Hot peppers come in many shapes and sizes, from round to cone-shaped to long and tapered.

Space plants 2 feet (60cm) apart in rows spaced at least 3 feet (90cm) apart.

Pepper stems are brittle and will break easily from a heavy crop of fruit. I like to surround my young pepper

plants with a cylinder of wide wire mesh, like a tomato tower, so that as the pepper grows it can push its side branches through the wire and become self-supporting.

Though aphids and Colorado potato beetles can colonize plants they are easily spotted and removed by hand or by spritzing the plants with an organic spray. Peppers suffer few other problems. Indeed, hot peppers are naturally repellent to insects and foraging animals, and you can make an effective organic repellent spray by using a juicer or mashing the fruit, straining it through a cheesecloth, and mixing it with water.

Sweet bell peppers are now available in a rainbow of colors, including handsome black varieties. Several of the blacks, like 'Islander', will change to yellow, then orange, and finally red.

Potatoes,

Irish

There are two kinds of potatoes commonly grown in North America—the Irish potato and the sweet potato. The Irish potato (which actually comes from South America) is a member of the nightshade family, while the sweet potato is a member of the morning glory family. You can follow a crop of Irish potatoes with a crop of sweet potatoes the next year, but avoid growing the same type of potato in one spot for two successive years. This is especially critical for Irish potatoes, which are susceptible to more diseases.

Irish potatoes are usually grown from either small tubers or from pieces of tuber with an "eye," or growing point, called a seed potato. Some varieties can be grown from seed, but the tubers and yields are never as large. In most areas 1 pound of seed potatoes will grow 15 pounds of edible tubers. There are early, mid-season, and late varieties: the earliest varieties mature in just 65 days; mid-season ones in 80 days; and late varieties in 90 to 100 days. Skin color varies from white through yellow, orange, pink, red, purple, and blue. Sometimes the skin color is carried through to the inside, but generally the inside of Irish potatoes is white.

There is a special group of Irish potatoes called Fingerlings. They have names like 'Russian Banana' and 'German Yellow' and they are considered the best-flavored and tenderest of all, with thin skins that require no peeling.

At Cedaridge Farm, white 'Katahdin' (a large, white, mid-season variety introduced in 1932) and red-skinned 'Red Norland' (the earliest red of all) are our favorites.

Plant potatoes in early spring, about 1 to 4 weeks before the last frost date, as they will tolerate mild frosts. Soil for potatoes should be well drained and preferably situated in raised beds. Sandy loam is the best. Alkaline soil produces scab disease, so maintain a slightly acidic soil if possible. Plant seed potatoes no deeper than 4 inches (10cm) from the base of the tuber. Space them 12 inches (30cm) apart, with at least 2 feet (60cm) of space between rows. Don't worry if some of your seed potatoes are already sprouted,

A harvest of variously colored Irish potatoes includes white 'Yukon Gold', red 'Caribe', and 'All-Blue'.

but handle them with care, as the sprouts break off easily. Discard any seed potatoes that are moldy or soft. If you cannot plant your seed potatoes as soon as you receive them, store them in a cool, dark place—the vegetable bin of a refrigerator is an excellent choice. Large tubers with plenty of eyes can be cut into several pieces; make sure to leave plenty of flesh around each eye. Where scab is a problem you may want to dust the tubers with sulphur before planting. Dusting with sulphur also guards against rot. To gain a few weeks you can presprout potatoes indoors by leaving them in wooden trays exposed to light and warmth. Once the pieces sprout, plant them deeply enough to bury the tuber, but with the green sprout poking through the soil.

When plants are 8 inches (20cm) high, hilling more soil around the base of the plants helps encourage higher yields. Mulching with black plastic, straw, or shredded leaves is also advisable to eliminate weeds. Potatoes will green when exposed to light. Since the green is a poison, be sure to keep plenty of mulch and/or soil over the roots of your plants. For maximum yield, use a booster foliar feed when the plant starts to blossom. Also, removing blossoms directs energy away from seed formation into tuber formation, resulting in higher yields.

Though you will have to wait until the potato stems have started to die down before harvesting your main crop of potatoes, it's possible to pick small "new" potatoes about the size of a golf ball within 40 to 60 days of planting. Just push your fingers into the soil around the stems and scrape away some soil to see the telltale bumps of extra tender, extra tasty new potatoes.

Harvest your main crop when the soil is dry and the stems are dead. If you plan to store the potatoes, leave them in the soil for 2 weeks after the vines have died to toughen the skins. Any small tubers can be placed in a basket and saved in a cool, dark place for use as the next season's seed potatoes. Saving seed potatoes from the most prolific clumps will produce the best results the following season. Some varieties—like 'Russett Burbank' and 'Butte' are naturally scab-resistant.

The Colorado potato beetle is the potato's worst pest. Both the larva (a grublike insect) and the adult (a black and white striped beetle) are ravenous feeders on leaves and stems, defoliating plants. Small populations can be hand picked; turn the leaves over to reveal yellow egg clusters. Beetle eggs and larvae overwinter in the soil, so crop rotation is essential. The biological control BT San Diego will control Colorado beetles and sprays of a rotenone/pyrethrum solution are effective too. Floating row covers will also protect potato plants from insect pests.

Since the leaves of the potato plant are poisonous and naturally repellent to foraging animals, deer will not touch them, but mice and gophers love to feast on tubers by digging underground. Special traps can catch them, and harmless corn snakes and cats are natural predators that keep down populations of these troublesome rodents.

Potatoes,
Sweet

'Beauregard' sweet potato has recently begun to rival 'Centennial' as the most popular variety for yield and good storageability.

Called yams in the South, sweet potatoes are an ancient food crop that will tolerate much hotter and drier conditions than Irish potatoes. Their culture is similar to Irish potatoes, but they tend to produce sprawling vines that makes a dense groundcover, and they need a longer growing season.

Sweet potatoes are generally orange in color, with orange skin, but they can also have red and yellow skins, and the flesh can vary from white to yellow to orange-red, depending on the variety. Sweet potatoes can be used the same way as Irish potatoes, though they have an almost sugary flavor when cooked.

Plants are grown from cuttings taken from a sprouting tuber. You can produce two dozen cuttings from one tuber by simply suspending a sweet potato tuber in a jar of water with the bottom half submerged (use toothpicks stuck in the tuber to keep the top half of the sweet potato above the jar's rim. Within 2 weeks green sprouts will emerge in clumps all around the tuber. These have roots formed at the base, and you simply break a clump off, tease the individual cuttings apart, and plant them outside after danger of frost.

If you buy plants from a mail order source or from a garden center they will be bundled. They can also look a sorry sight, with droopy, wilted leaves. Usually this wilted look disappears once the plants are set into their planting stations, spaced at least 12 inches (30cm) apart in rows spaced 3 feet (90cm) apart.

Sweet potatoes prefer sandy, well-drained soils, and especially soil that is raised up a foot or more. Avoid high nitrogen fertilizers, as this promotes too much leafy growth at the expense of tubers. Instead, use a high-phosphorus and potash fertilizer. Indeed, most sweet potato problems are the result of poor or waterlogged soil where fungal diseases can cause serious skin blemishes and rot. Soil nematodes can also cause scarring and cracking of tubers. Where soil is heavy or low-lying, build up a wide raised bed specially for sweet potatoes, and add sand. Where nematodes are a problem sterilize the soil before planting, or interplant with marigolds as a repellent.

The best sweet potato variety is 'Beauregard'—an aggressive vining plant that produces large, fat tubers with orange skin and orange-yellow flesh. 'Beauregard,' developed by Louisiana State University, will store for up to 6 months at room temperature.

Pumpkins

New short-vine pumpkin varieties such as 'Cinderella' are ideal for small gardens since these varieties don't require additional space to accommodate the rambling vines of most pumpkins.

Pumpkins are simply a type of squash, and like all winter squashes, they require a lot of space to grow. Direct-seed after danger of frost, planting the seeds 1 inch (2.5cm) deep, 6 feet (180cm) apart, with 6 feet (180cm) between rows. Starting seeds in peat pots 4 weeks before outdoor planting produces seedlings with a good head start. The transplants are then set into the garden into a humus-rich, fertile soil (especially one supplemented with well-decomposed dairy or stable manure). A deeply spaded, crumbly clay loam works best; cover the soil with black plastic to keep it warm. Regular watering is essential because it is water that contributes most to a pumpkin's weight gain. The most important nutrient is nitrogen, which promotes healthy leaf growth—-the bigger the vine, the bigger the pumpkin can grow. Phosphorus is also important because it promotes early flowering and fruit formation, and potash aids in disease resistance and overall vigor.

Pumpkins set two kinds of flowers: male and female. Only the females set fruit (you can recognize a female by looking under the flower—females will have a baby pumpkin), but they must receive pollen from a male. To get an early fruit set you must play the part of a bee and examine the flowers each morning until you find a female (the males always appear first), then pick a male blossom and rub the powdery "nose" on the shiny nose of the female. This effects pollination.

Continue hand pollinating as many female flowers as possible over a period of several weeks until several of the little pumpkins are the size of a grapefruit, then examine them for the thickest stem and the best shape. Since pumpkins take nourishment from the vine through their stems, a healthy, thick stem is vital. After selecting the best specimen, remove all other fruit so that the plant's energy goes into making just one gigantic specimen.

Pumpkins should be harvested before the first frost and laid in the sun or in a warm, airy place until the shells are hard. Store them in a cool, dry place and they should keep well into the winter.

Radishes

'French Breakfast' radishes have long, blunt, red roots and white tips, plus a crisp, icy flavor.

Except for sprouting seeds, like cress, which can mature in 10 days, there is no faster-growing vegetable than 'Cherry Belle' radish, which won an All-America Award for its rapid maturity and excellent quality. From direct-seeding into the garden in early spring, 'Cherry Belle' is ready to harvest in just 20 days! The key to this rapid growth is cool weather and a moist but well-drained soil. Poor flavor in radishes is usually due to stress from heat or lack of moisture.

In addition to the round, red radishes that are most common among home gardeners, there are white, carrot-shaped radishes ('Icicle'—30 days), bicolored radishes

('French Breakfast'—25 days), a rainbow mix ('Easter Egg'—25 days), which includes orange, pink, and purple; plus large-rooted radishes like 'China Rose' (55 days) and 'Black Spanish' (55 days).

Grow radishes in spring or fall, planting several small crops in succession. Because of their rapid growth, radishes are ideal for interplanting with slower-growing plants. Plant seeds ¼ inch (0.6cm) deep, spacing seeds of the small-rooted types 1 inch (2.5cm) apart in rows spaced 12 inches (30cm) apart. Seeds may be sown outdoors several weeks before the last frost date.

Above: 'Cherry Belle' is the earliest-maturing radish—ready to harvest in just 20 days. Right: 'Valentine' rhubarb must be grown from divisions to retain its deep red skin color.

Rhubarb

The answer to substantial yields of rhubarb is regular amounts of water, as well as fertile, well-drained soil that contains plenty of humus, particularly garden compost or well-decomposed animal manure (notably cow manure). Although rhubarb is a hardy perennial vegetable that is easily grown from seed to provide worthwhile yields the following season, the best rhubarb is grown from root divisions, or clones created by tissue-culture. That is because seed-grown plants are variable, while roots and clones produce an exact replica of the parent.

The variety 'Valentine' presently has the deepest red color of any rhubarb and is the sweetest of all rhubarbs (though sugar is still needed to sweeten it sufficiently after cooking). Most rhubarb varieties show their deep red coloring only at the bottom of the stalks, but 'Valentine' shows it all the way up the stalks. **Take care not to eat any of the green part of the leaf as it contains a toxin.**

Plant the roots 3 inches (7.5cm) deep so the crown is just below the soil surface, spacing plants 3 feet (90cm) apart in rows spaced 3 feet (90cm) apart. If any flower stems start to sprout from the center, prune them out. You want all the plant's energy directed to the stalks, rather than to seed formation.

To prepare rhubarb for cooking, peel the stalks, cut into 1- to 2-inch (2.5 to 5cm) segments and steam or boil until they are tender and moist. Add maple syrup or sugar to sweeten. It's also delicious when sweetened and baked into pies.

Shallots

Shallots, an essential ingredient in French cooking, have a slightly tangy taste similar to mild onions.

If a French chef had to choose between shallots and onions, shallots would surely be the winner, because their flavor is both classic and consistent, while onions can vary considerably from mild to hot depending on variety and growing conditions. No onion can match the perfect piquancy of shallots, and that is why shallots are favored for English pickles, preserved in jars of malt vinegar.

Shallots are planted in spring from small bulbs, with one bulb to a planting station. Plant them 12 inches (30cm) apart, with the base of the bulb in the soil and the top protruding. By the end of summer that one bulb will produce a dozen progeny, which are harvested as soon as the leaves die down.

Brush away all the soil and place the bulbs on screens to cure for a day. Then store shallots in a dark, cool, frost-free place on shelves. The outer, reddish-brown skin is peeled before cooking to reveal a white interior. Use shallots whole as pickles, or chop them fine to flavor soups, sautées, vinegars, salads, or any dishes where a classic onion flavor is desired.

Spinach

'Melody' spinach won an All-America Award for its abundant, dark green, succulent, heavily textured leaves.

This easily grown, fast-maturing leafy green is excellent alone as a salad or mixed with lettuce, and it makes a nutritious side dish when cooked or steamed. Its only serious demand is a cool growing period. The seed will germinate at cool temperatures (40°F [3°C] or higher), though I prefer to pregerminate the seed indoors in a moist paper towel and then plant the split or swollen seeds outdoors 6 inches (15cm) apart in rows spaced 12 inches (30cm) apart. When direct-seeding, plant seeds ¼ inch (0.6cm) deep. Plants withstand even moderately severe frosts, so outdoor planting can occur 4 weeks before the last spring frost date.

An inexpensive open-pollinated spinach is 'Bloomsdale Long Standing'. If sown in early September, plants will make strong growth, and even in northern gardens will usually survive winter to produce an extra-early spring harvest. An excellent hybrid variety is 'Melody' (42 days), which produces lush plants with blistered, dark green leaves, and which matures earlier than the regular kind. Developed in Holland, 'Melody' is an All-America winner.

New Zealand spinach is a low, spreading plant that tolerates summer heat better than traditional spinach. Plant both kinds to enjoy spinach throughout the season.

Spinach,
New Zealand

While regular spinach is a cool-season vegetable, New Zealand spinach is a warm-weather crop, germinating when the soil is warm and frost-free. The plants grow especially quickly during warm weather, and seed germination is speeded by first soaking the hard-coated seeds overnight in lukewarm water before direct-seeding. Thin the seedlings to stand 8 inches (20cm) apart in rows 2 feet (60cm) apart. Within 55 days the plants will form a dense, spreading mat of thick, succulent, pointed leaves. Pick the topmost whorl of young leaves for tenderest flavor. Use New Zealand spinach raw in salads or cooked like spinach.

Squash,
Summer

Summer squash is extremely easy to grow, and yields are quicker than for winter squash. The two most popular summer squashes are zucchini and vegetable spaghetti.

Vegetable spaghetti grows on a vine that produces large, cylindrical fruits. These can be either pale yellow or golden at maturity, depending on the variety, and they mature in 90 to 100 days. The fruits will store for long periods indoors, and they have become a popular vegetable in supermarket produce aisles.

Vegetable spaghetti is best grown along raised beds 2 feet (60cm) wide, or trained to climb up a trellis or other strong support. The pumpkinlike seeds should be planted 2 inches (5cm) deep in fertile soil after all danger of frost is past. Planting through black plastic increases yields. Space plants at least 4 feet (1.2m) apart in rows 4 feet (1.2m) apart, and allow the vines to knit together.

To avoid wilt disease keep the vines free of cucumber beetles and control borers. Rotenone/pyrethrum organic sprays will keep their populations down.

To prepare vegetable spaghetti, simply pierce the skin with a fork and cook in the oven for 45 minutes at 450°F (232°C). Then slice the fruit down the middle with a sharp knife and scoop out the central cluster of seeds with a spoon. Fluff up the center with a fork. It will unravel just like strands of spaghetti. Serve hot with your favorite spaghetti sauce, like meatballs and marinara sauce or—my favorite—parsley butter and clams.

Zucchini squash and a host of similar squashes—like pattypan squash (which is scallop shaped), and crooknecks (also called swan's neck)—are variations in shape of the same species. Zucchini is by far the most popular because it is so easy to grow, easy to prepare for cooking, and quick to yield a crop.

Unlike vegetable spaghetti, which grows as a sprawling vine, zucchinis, crooknecks, and pattypans grow bushy,

When cooked, the interior of spaghetti squash, or vegetable spaghetti, unravels to make a good substitute for pasta.

and need the same spacing. The seed can be direct-sown into the garden after all danger of frost, and within 50 days it's possible to be harvesting baby zucchinis. However, it's important to realize that the zucchinis develop only from female flowers and standard varieties are male dominant, meaning the male flowers come first, and there are more male flowers than females. You can tell the difference between the males and females by looking beneath the flower—the females have an immature baby zucchini already formed. Also, the center of the female flower has a shiny "nose." Males have only a slender stalk under the flower, and the center of the flower has a powdery "nose." Though insects usually effect the transfer of pollen from the male to the female, a surer method of ensuring an early fruit set is to pick a male flower and rub its powdery nose on as many female flowers as possible. If the baby zucchini starts to enlarge then you know the pollination has been successful. If it turns black, the reverse is true.

In recent years plant breeders have been able to produce hybrid zucchinis that are female dominant. Some seed companies call them "all-female" (a term also used to describe female-dominant cucumbers), though the plants will set a small percentage of male flowers. Two zucchinis that I heartily recommend are a green hybrid zucchini, 'Richgreen', and a yellow-fruited hybrid called 'Gold Rush'. Just two plants will keep a family of four well supplied with zucchinis.

Earliest and highest yields are possible by planting through black plastic and loading the soil with good garden compost. Take special care when harvesting zucchini. Use a sharp knife to cut the fruit where it is attached to the stem. Pull the knife up from under the fruit, since by cutting down you may sever the vine and kill the plant.

The most important point to remember about zucchini is that the fruit should be picked when it is small (no more than 6 inches [15cm] in length); otherwise the plant quickly exhausts itself. When small, the fruit are exceedingly tender and can be eaten raw, sliced thin into salads, or cooked for just a few minutes to make a delicious side dish. There are so many ways to use zucchini squashes that several books are devoted entirely to this versatile squash.

In addition to the fruits, squash blossoms are tasty when dipped in a breadcrumb batter and lightly fried. The blossoms are not edible for long. They swell up in the early morning, open fully during the dawn hours, and close by midmorning. Flowers harvested early, before they open, have the best consistency and tastiest flavor.

'Richgreen' zucchini squash, a green hybrid variety, sets a higher percentage of fruit because it has more female flowers than traditional varieties.

Squash,
Winter

Winter squash (also called fall squash) should not be harvested when immature, but allowed to grow to full size and develop a hard shell. Winter squashes are a quintessential North American vegetable, cultivated by the Indians long before Europeans began colonizing the continent. The most popular are acorns and buttercups. Though these normally require lots of space to develop their vigorous, sprawling vines some spacesaving bushy types—such as 'Butterbush' and 'Early Acorn Hybrid' (both 75 days)—have been developed. They are not as heavy yielding or large-fruited as the vining kind but are well worth the smaller space they occupy—you can even grow them in whisky half-barrels.

For vining winter squash, sow seeds directly into the garden along raised beds, with plants spaced at least 6 feet (1.8m) apart in rows spaced 4 feet (1.2m) apart so the vines intermingle. The bush kinds can be spaced 3 feet (90cm) apart in rows spaced 3 feet (90cm) apart. Plant several seeds together, 1½ inches (3.7cm) deep, and thin to the strongest seedling.

Highest yields are possible by growing in soil that has good drainage and is loaded with compost. In fact, an old compost pile is an ideal place to grow vining types of

winter squash. As with summer squash, highest yields are possible by planting through black plastic. To harvest, take a serrated knife and saw through the tough stem, leaving at least an inch of hard stem attached to the fruit. This portion of stem will deter rot if you plan on storing the fruits for any length of time. Store in a frost-free, dark space on wooden boards or screens. Clean fruit will keep for up to 6 months.

The flavor of winter squash varies according to the variety, but most taste like a sweet potato when cooked. All contain a seed cavity that is easily scooped out with a spoon, leaving a cup-shaped depression. Fill the depression with maple syrup during cooking for a wonderful combination of flavors.

This collection of squash includes acorn squash, striped cushaw, Boston marrow, butternut, Turk's turban, pumpkin, and vegetable spaghetti.

Tomatoes

The luscious, lovely tomato is North America's most widely planted home garden vegetable. Today, it is estimated that there are at least three thousand species and varieties of tomato in cultivation. Ask any home gardener what he looks for in a tomato for his backyard, and the answer is likely to be "good flavor." Of course, flavor is an intangible element. What most home gardeners look for is a tomato that is meaty, firm, smooth-skinned, and sweet, rather than watery, insipid, misshapen, or sour. To achieve that delectable combination, choose the right variety, provide the right growing conditions, harvest at the peak of ripeness, and eat the fruit as soon as possible after peak ripeness so it doesn't lose flavor during long storage.

A lot of gardeners equate flavor with size, thinking that small or medium-sized tomatoes taste best. Actually, some giant-fruited varieties can compete successfully in flavor tests. It is most important to choose mainly American-bred tomatoes, staying away from foreign-bred varieties. I've found that varieties such as 'Siberian',

'Marmande', and 'Sub Arctic' (from Europe and Canada) are not worth growing. A far better all-purpose tomato is 'Supersonic' (medium-sized), 'Burpee's Big Early' (large-sized), and 'Supersteak VF Hybrid' (giant-sized). In the cherry-size class, try 'Sweet 100' and 'Sunray' (which is orange-fruited)—these not only bear an enormous amount of fruit, they are sugary sweet. The cherry types are a cinch to grow; it's the large-fruited varieties that require some special tips to promote a full-bodied, luscious flavor.

First, when setting out transplants (whether grown from seed yourself or purchased from a garden center), choose stocky transplants. Avoid any plants that are stretched, already fruiting, or a yellowish green. These are signs of stress, and a stressed tomato that has been set out will take a long time to overcome transplant shock. Plant the roots of healthy plants deep (more roots will sprout up the lower stem; the bigger the root system underground, the more nutrients will reach the fruit to ensure good flavor).

Water daily until the plants are well established, and then water every 3 days in the absence of natural rainfall.

A harvest of home-grown tomatoes features cherry-size 'Sungold', 'Yellow Pear', and 'Yellow Perfection', as well as giant red 'Supersteak' and 'Early Cascade'. Watch fruit carefully as it matures in order to harvest at the peak of ripeness.

Left: The Italian pear tomato 'Roma' is especially good for canning, allowing you to enjoy the taste of sun-ripened tomatoes throughout the year. Below: 'Yellow Perfection' displays its globe-shaped fruit.

Though tomatoes demand a fertile soil with excellent drainage, it is moisture in the soil that enables the plant to absorb nutrients in soluble form (through its roots), convert those nutrients into sugars, and pass those sugars into the fruit.

Always wait until after the last frost date to plant tomatoes, since they are damaged by frost, and if a late frost threatens be sure to protect them through the night with plastic cones called "hot caps," which are available from garden centers. To help warm up the soil (tomatoes love a warm soil), place a sheet of black plastic around each plant. The few degrees of temperature it raises the soil can make a drastic difference in plant performance. Also, the plastic will help conserve soil moisture and prevent competition from weeds. Don't mulch with an organic material such as straw or shredded leaves, as this will lower the soil temperature.

For a tomato plant to give its very best, the soil should be slightly acidic and enriched with a high-phosphorous fertilizer such as 10-15-10. If you load your soil with a high-nitrogen fertilizer (such as animal manure), you may find that your tomatoes take forever to ripen because the nutrients are directed toward the leaves rather than the fruit. Calcium, a trace element, is also important for healthy, flavorful tomatoes. A little lime or some crushed eggshells will add the required calcium. Without a supply of calcium, your tomato plants may develop a disease called blossom-end rot, which causes the bottom of the fruit to turn black, rendering the entire fruit distasteful. Though tomato plants relish full sun, exposing the fruits to too much direct sunlight (which usually happens when you trim away the plant's leaves) may cause the fruit to develop a pale patch, known as sunscald. This renders the fruit insipid.

Inspect fruit carefully as it ripens. Though tomatoes are good to eat when they are a scarlet color, with green shoulders, it is best to wait an extra day for them to turn a deep red and to color completely while still firm.

Use the fruit as soon as possible after picking. To prolong firmness, keep fruit cool. The longer you store a ripe tomato, the poorer the flavor. When frost threatens to end the harvest, pick all mature green fruit (any tomatoes that look full size but are still green). Keep these in a warm room, such as the kitchen, and they will continue to ripen, unlike many other fruits that stop ripening once they are picked.

Tomato-Potato

Tomatoes above ground, potatoes below—this amazing plant is created by grafting a tomato plant onto a potato tuber so that the two grow together in the same space.

Several years ago I read in the *Royal Horticultural Society Journal* (the official publication of the prestigious British garden society) that it was possible to graft a tomato plant onto a potato plant! When I tried to find out how this was done I hit a brick wall. In theory it was possible, since tomatoes and potatoes are closely related (both are members of the Solanaceae family), but in practice it simply didn't seem possible.

One night, in my sleep, I suddenly realized how the graft could be done! I grew some tomato plants in special cone-shaped plugs of soil and cut a hole right through a potato tuber to make a snug fit for the plug. I then tested six plants of different variety combinations. The results were astounding. Not only did I get a bountiful harvest of juicy tomatoes on the tomato part of the graft, but lots of plump potatoes on the potato part.

If you follow my instructions carefully, I can promise you the most thrilling growing experience of a lifetime—'Red Pontiac' potatoes below ground and red, ripe 'Pixie' tomatoes above ground within 58 days of planting. Here's what you do: select a potato tuber about the size of a lemon; take an apple corer or a sharp knife and core a 1-inch (2.5cm)-wide hole in the potato; and poke a hole 1-inch (2.5cm)-wide, right through until you can see daylight. Then take a tomato transplant that has been grown in a small pot, slip out the root ball, and trim it down to fit the hole in the potato. Push the tomato plant all the way down so that the tomato roots poke through the bottom of the hole in the potato. Plant outdoors after all danger of frost, with the potato tuber just below the soil surface and the tomato foliage above the soil, and water well. In the succeeding weeks, if at any time the potato stems look like they will suffocate the tomato, just prune some back so there is always light reaching the tomato. The soil should be fertile and the plant should be watered whenever a week goes by without a good soaking rainfall.

When the tomatoes are ripe call everyone in the neighborhood to watch you harvest your tomato-potato. Simply take a fork and ceremoniously dig into the soil to loosen the potato roots. Then yank the entire plant out of the ground and there will be screams of delight and astonishment as the plump, shiny potatoes appear miraculously among the tomato roots.

Turnips *and* Swedes

Turnip 'Tokyo Cross' has round, white, sweetly flavored roots.

In Scotland, turnips are called "neeps," and nothing tastes better than a Scottish turnip, fertilized with well-decomposed cow manure and blessed with cold rain almost daily. In those conditions you can grow a turnip from seed to harvest in 35 days! Closely related to turnips are swedes, which take much longer to grow (up to 90 days). But

'Purple Top' turnips can be globe-shaped (like these) or flattened, depending on the strain of seed. The tops of turnips are also edible when cooked as greens—use them as you would spinach.

swedes store more easily, especially when waxed. 'Laurentian,' the most popular variety, has a sweet, orange interior.

The best turnips are bred in Japan, where some of the hybrids are unbelievably sweet. Their leading breeder, Takii, has won two All-America Awards for turnips—for 'Tokyo Cross' (35 days) and 'Just Right' (70 days). 'Tokyo Cross' is white with a perfect globe shape. Because of its earliness it is perfect for growing in spring, and is at its sweetest when the size of a golf ball. 'Just Right' should be allowed to remain in the garden longer to grow larger—to about the size of a tennis ball. It grows best from a midsummer sowing to mature during cool fall weather. Both varieties have edible green leaves that can be cooked like spinach.

Turnip seeds are small and round like cabbage seeds. Sow them ¼ inch (0.6cm) deep, and thin the resulting seedlings to stand 3 inches (7.5cm) apart. Crowding will restrict root development, producing deformed roots instead of plump, rounded ones, so allow at least 12 inches (30cm) between rows.

For best flavor grow turnips in fertile, sandy soil and ensure that they are not stressed for moisture. Any check in growth from a dry spell or hot weather can turn them fibrous and bitter. Frost extenders such as floating row covers and plastic tunnels can carry turnips through winter months, until the ground freezes. 'Just Right' is highly cold-tolerant. 'Purple-Top White Globe' (55 days) is a very popular standby with good visual appeal because of its purple and white coloration, but it isn't nearly as sweetly flavored as the Japanese hybrids.

Root maggots (the same pests that can attack radishes and cabbage) can cause blemishes to turnips. Floating row covers are an effective organic control.

About
the
Author

Derek Fell is a writer and photographer who specializes in gardening, with an emphasis on step-by-step gardening concepts and garden design. He lives in Bucks County, Pennsylvania, at historic Cedaridge Farm, Tinicum Township, where he cultivates extensive award-winning flower and vegetable gardens that have been featured in *Architectural Digest, Garden Design, Beautiful Gardens, Gardens Illustrated, American Nurseryman,* and *Mid-Atlantic Country* magazines. Born and educated in England, he first worked for seven years with Europe's largest seed company, then moved to Pennsylvania in 1964 to work for Burpee Seeds as their catalog manager, a position he held for six years before taking on duties as executive director of the All-America Selections (the national seed trials) and the National Garden Bureau (an information office sponsored by the American seed industry). Now the author of more than fifty garden books and calendars, he has traveled widely throughout North America, also documenting gardens in Europe, Africa, New Zealand, and Asia. His most recent books are *Renoir's Garden* (Simon & Schuster), *The Impressionist Garden* (Crown), *500 Perennial Garden Ideas* (Simon & Schuster), and *In the Garden with Derek* (Camino Books).

A frequent contributor to *Architectural Digest* and *Woman's Day* magazines, Derek Fell is the winner of more awards from the Garden Writers Association of America than any other garden writer. He also worked as a consultant on gardening to the White House during the Ford Administration.

Wall calendars, greeting cards, and art posters featuring Derek Fell's photography are published worldwide. He has lectured on photography and the gardens of the great Impressionist painters at numerous art museums, including the Smithsonian Institution in Washington, D.C.; the Philadelphia Museum of Art, the Barnes Foundation, Philadelphia; and the Denver Art Museum, Colorado. He is also host of a regular garden show for the QVC cable television shopping channel, entitled *Step-by-Step Gardening,* which is plugged into fifty million homes.

Fell's highly acclaimed *Step-by-Step Gardening* mail-order perennial plant catalogs for Spring Hill Nurseries (North America's largest mail-order nursery) reach an audience of home gardeners estimated to be more than three million in spring and autumn. He is a former president of the Hobby Greenhouse Association, a former director of the Garden Writers Association of America, the president of the International Test Gardeners Association, and a cofounder of the American Gardening Association.

A complete list of published works follows.

Books by Derek Fell
(asterisk indicates coauthorship)

The White House Vegetable Garden. 1976, Exposition.

House Plants for Fun & Profit. 1978, Bookworm.

How to Photograph Flowers, Plants, & Landscapes. 1980, HP Books.

Vegetables: How to Select, Grow, and Enjoy. 1982, HP Books.

Annuals: How to Select, Grow, and Enjoy. 1983, HP Books.

Deerfield: An American Garden Through Four Seasons. 1986, Pidcock Press.

Trees & Shrubs. 1986, HP Books.

Garden Accents. 1987, Henry Holt (*Inspired Garden* in the United Kingdom).

*Discover Anguilla. 1988, Caribbean Concepts.

*Home Landscaping. 1988, Simon & Schuster.

The One-Minute Gardener. 1988, Running Press.

A Kid's First Gardening Book. 1989, Running Press.

*Three Year Garden Journal. 1989, Starwood.

*Ornamental Grass Gardening. 1989, HP Books.

*The Complete Garden Planning Manual. 1989, HP Books.

The Essential Gardener. 1990, Crown.

Essential Roses. 1990, Crown.

Essential Annuals. 1990, Crown.

Essential Bulbs. 1990, Crown.

Essential Herbs. 1990, Crown.

Essential Perennials. 1990, Crown.

Essential Shrubs. 1990, Crown.

The Easiest Flower to Grow. 1990, Ortho.

*550 Home Landscaping Ideas. 1991, Simon & Schuster.

Renoir's Garden. 1991, Simon & Schuster.

Beautiful Bucks County. 1991, Cedaridge.

* The Encyclopedia of Ornamental Grasses. 1992, Smithmark.

The Encyclopedia of Flowers. 1993, Smithmark.

Garden Guide: Annuals. 1993, Smithmark.

Garden Guide: Perennials. 1993, Smithmark.

Garden Guide: Bulbs. 1993, Smithmark.

Garden Guide: Roses. 1993, Smithmark.

*550 Perennial Garden Ideas. 1993, Simon & Schuster.

The Impressionist Garden. 1994, Crown.

*Practical Gardening. 1995, Friedman/Fairfax.

*Gardens of Philadelphia & the Delaware Valley. 1995, Temple University Press.

The Pennsylvania Gardener. 1995, Camino Books.

In the Garden with Derek. 1995, Camino Books.

Calendars

Great Gardens (Portal)

The Impressionist Garden (Portal)

The Gardening Year (Portal)

Perennials (Starwood)

Flowering Shrubs (Starwood)

Flowering Bulbs (Starwood)

Northeast Gardens Calendar (Starwood)

Mid-Atlantic Gardens Calendar (Starwood)

Southern Gardens Calendar (Starwood)

California Gardens Calendar (Starwood)

Pacific Northwest Gardens Calendar (Starwood)

Art Posters

Deerfield Garden (Portal)

Spring Garden (Portal)

Monet's Bridge (Portal)

Sources

for Seeds and Plants

The following reputable companies produce mail-order catalogs, most of which are available free of charge.

W. Atlee Burpee & Co.
300 Park Avenue
Warminster, PA 18974

Excellent source of vegetable seeds and plants, many developed by the company's plant breeders working for home garden varieties.

The Cook's Garden
Box 535
Londonderry, VT 05148

Comprehensive listing of vegetable seeds; specialists in salad greens such as lettuce.

Gurney's Seed & Nursery Co.
110 Capitol Street
Yankton, SD 57079

Large selection of popular and hard-to-find vegetable seeds and plants.

Harris Seeds
3670 Buffalo Road
Rochester, NY 14624

Specialists in vegetables grown from seed, many developed by their own breeding program.

Johnny's Selected Seeds
Foss Hill Road
Albion, ME 04910-9371

Cold-hardy and short-season varieties a specialty. Company maintains extensive test gardens worth visiting.

Earl May Seed & Nursery Co.
208 North Elm Street
Shenandoah, IA 51603

Good source of vegetables grown from seed and plants.

Geo. W. Park Seed Co.
Highway 254 North
Greenwood, SC 29647

Extensive vegetable seed section. The company runs an extensive test garden that is worth visiting.

Piedmont Plant Company
Box 424
Albany, GA 31703

Suppliers of vegetable plants; no seeds.

Pinetree Garden Seeds
New Gloucester, ME 04260

Compared to other mail-order sources, their prices for vegetable seeds are consistently the lowest.

Seeds of Change
Box 5700
Santa Fe, NM 87506

A relatively young company appealing to organic gardeners. A big emphasis on heirloom vegetable varieties.

Shepherd's Garden Seeds
30 Irene Street
Torrington, CT 06790

This California company now operates from New England. Emphasis on European varieties.

Stokes Seeds Inc.
39 James Street
St. Catherine's, Ontario L2R 6R6
Canada

A first-rate vegetable seed house with a Buffalo shipping office. The company maintains one of the world's best trial gardens.

Territorial Seed Co.
20 Palmer Ave.
Cottage Grove, OR 97424

Specialist vegetable seed supplier for the Pacific Northwest.

Thompson & Morgan
Box 1308
Jackson, NJ 08527

An old, established British seed company with many distinctive vegetable varieties available nowhere else.

Tomato Growers Supply Co.
Box 2237
Fort Myers, FL 33902

Extensive listing of tomatoes and peppers, with many heirloom varieties.

Twilley Seed Co.
Box 65
Trevose, PA 19047

Excellent listing of vegetable seeds, many of them exclusives developed by the company. A favorite source among Amish gardeners.

Sources

f o r   T o o l s   a n d   S u p p l i e s

The following companies produce mail order catalogs with mostly organic remedies for pest control and fertilizing.

Gardener's Supply
128 Intervale Road
Burlington, VT 05401

Colorful catalog featuring many useful garden aids such as seed-starting supplies, plus organically approved fertilizer and insect controls.

Gardens Alive
5100 Schenley Place
Lawrenceburg, IN 47025

Full color catalog with North America's biggest selection of organic pest controls and fertilizers.

International Irrigation Systems
1555 Third Avenue
Niagara Falls, NY 14304

Inexpensive drip irrigation systems, including disposable and permanent subsurface systems.

Natural Solutions
1 Nature's Way
New Castle, VA 24127-0305

Complete line of organic pest controls and plant foods.

Nitron Formula
4605 Johnson Road
Fayetteville, AK 72702

Organic plant food systems, both liquid and granular to feed vegetable gardens, plus organic pest controls.

Ringer Research
6860 Flying Cloud Drive
Eden Prairie, MN 55344

Extensive range of organic fertilizers and pest controls.

Index